It's not the farts
that kill—
it's the smell!

I met Lars-Olof Nilsson while serving as Ambassador of Slovenia to the Kingdom of Sweden. Many discussions with him revealed his special feeling for people and nature, and I have noticed his language proficiency and communication skills. Diplomacy and international relations are all about language, communication, and understanding of your interlocutor. For this reason, I do congratulate the author on this extraordinary book, which I would recommend not only to all the members of the foreign diplomatic community serving in the Kingdom of Sweden and using English and Swedish for official communication. I also recommend this excellent book to other scholars and experts studying the Swedish language and trying to master it. Lars-Olof Nilsson's book will help them, sometimes in a fun way, to better discover Swedish and English language similarities and differences and will certainly assist them to better understand the deeper meaning of the Swedish language.

TONE KAJZER, former Ambassador of Slovenia to the Kingdom of Sweden (serving from 2013 to 2018)

Lars-Olof Nilsson's book is an interesting mini-dictionary of English and Swedish. It is a type of lexicon that is useful, practical, and amusing to read. We suffer from false friends, who are not friends indeed when in need. They seem to be good friends but in practice they are not. But it is difficult to tell who is a good friend and who is a bad friend; only practice speaks. English and Swedish are friends, i.e., speakers or writers may see the two languages sharing some common ground with so many vocabularies having close affinity in terms of spelling and pronunciation. Lars-Olof Nilsson shows that these vocabularies may not be good friends. They are false, i.e., Swedish speakers of English, or English speakers of Swedish for that matter, should be careful when using them as they may lead to serious failures in communication. He has provided an inventory of more than 400 most commonly used Swedish vocabularies that fall under the category of 'false friends' with explanations of their meanings in both languages. I commend the effort and recommend the book. It is indeed a practical guide to not getting caught in the trap of 'false friends' when speaking or writing English.

LEON YOUSIF BARKHO, Professor of Media and Communication Sciences, University of Sharjah, UAE; founder and editor of *Journal of Applied Journalism and Media Studies*

For anyone whose work involves English and Swedish, is studying one or both languages, or just enjoys using both—this book is essential reading. It is presented in a way that simply captivates your interest and guarantees laughter. The author has distilled a lifetime of teaching into material that will help to reduce the sometimes embarrassing linguistic errors by making the wrong assumptions about usage.

While I speak both English, French, and Swedish fluently, and have for many years, I still learned so much about all three languages—and discovered that I had been using some terms in Swedish incorrectly. This would be an ideal companion for anyone who can speak Swedish and English reasonably well and is sufficiently humble to admit that there is much they do not know and would like to improve. Your time will be rewarded.

H. DENNIS BEAVER, Bakersfield, CA, attorney and syndicated legal affairs columnist writing for Kiplinger.com

Lars-Olof Nilsson's book *It's not the farts that kill—it's the smell!* is a must read for any Swedish-speaking person who wants to excel in the treacherous English-speaking world. If you are a high-flying businessperson making deals in English or a Swedish person living in an English-speaking country, or simply someone interested in language, this book is for you. Nilsson's list of "false friends and other treacherous words" is enormous, and each one is followed by a historical background or explanation. Not only does this book educate, but it is also a fun and humorous read—a great addition to anyone's home library!!!

PETER HILTON, Lead Negotiator, Ministry of Indigenous Relations and Reconciliation, Kamloops, BC, Canada

What a useful book this is! It is a book that will be of great help to many of us translators. I recognized many of the words and phrases that have been imported into Swedish that we believe have the same meaning as in English. It is a very interesting and at the same time fun book. What I like most is that the author gives practical examples, comparisons, and explanations. *Helt klart en superbra bok!* Clearly an awesome book!

DANNI STRAZAR, translator, Stockholm, Sweden

Whether or not you like this book and believe that others may benefit from it, you can write a review on the book's page on Amazon. In the **Customer Reviews** section, select **Write a product review**. Select a star rating and, if you like, add a comment and select **Submit**.

It's not the farts that kill– it's the smell!

False friends and other treacherous words in English-Swedish communication

Lars-Olof Nilsson

Medium Text & Bild

Copyright © Lars-Olof Nilsson, 2024

All rights reserved.

Published in Sweden by Medium Text & Bild, Vevslupsgränd 2,
SE-553 30 Jönköping, medium@bahnhof.se.

The title of this book is used with permission from Norwegian comedian and impersonator Kristian Valen, who coined the expression in a skit on the internet.

No part of this publication may be reproduced in any form, or by any means, electronic or mechanical, including photocopying, recording, or any information browsing, storage, or retrieval system, without permission in writing from the publisher.

Although this book is designed to provide accurate information in regard to the subject matter covered, the publisher and the author assume no responsibility for errors, inaccuracies, omissions, or any other inconsistencies herein.

First edition, 2024
ISBN 978-91-527-9657-3

For Karolina
—*my true friend*

Table of contents

Preface ----- xi

Introduction ----- xv

What are false friends? ----- 1

… and what are treacherous words? ----- 3

A note on Swedish forms of some English loanwords ----- 4

Periods in the history of languages ----- 5

English–Swedish false friends ----- 7

Conclusion ----- 218

Preface

Years ago, not to say decades ago, I was standing outside a pub in northern Wales talking to another young man. For reasons that I cannot remember, the conversation turned into philosophy (perhaps I just wanted to show off how much I thought I knew), and I mentioned *the categorical imperative*, an ethical principle formulated by the German philosopher Immanuel Kant. 'You know Kant?', I asked, and I noticed that my interlocutor had a strange look on his face. At that time, I did not know any English so-called four-letter words, and he was apparently not acquainted with German philosophers. (The four-letter word in question, rhyming with Kant, can be found among words beginning with C in this book.)

When words in different languages have the same pronunciation and/or spelling but very different meanings, we call them false friends. Often, they lead to a bit of confusion or some embarrassment, but little more. However, they have the potential of causing far more serious problems in the realm of international communication.

Even if the English and Swedish languages are related, there are numerous similar-looking words in the two languages with very different meanings, which may lead to misunderstandings.

Imagine that, as a business executive, you are negotiating a deal with a potential partner in Sweden. You get an email with the following lines:

> We are having problems with reparations in our fabric. I have just handed in my rapport to the VD. We have sent reclamations to the entrepreneur, who wanted a higher provision, and must eventually find another building society.

> Through a slump I found a serious fault in the contract. I am afraid the concurrents in our branch will take advantage of our situation. After the fusion two years ago, our concern became more effective, especially at our filial in Gothenburg, but the actual situation worries me, especially since it will soon be semester time. Idle problems!

Understandably, you get confused. This is what the writer wanted to say:

> We are having problems with repairs in our factory. I have just handed in my report to the CEO. We have sent complaints to the contractor, who wanted a higher commission, and will possibly have to find another construction company. By coincidence I found a serious mistake in the contract. I am afraid the competitors in our industry will take advantage of our situation. After the merger two years ago, our group became more efficient, especially at our branch in Gothenburg, but the current situation worries me, especially since vacations are coming up. Nothing but problems!

When it comes to English proficiency among non-native speakers, Sweden usually ranks among the top three countries in the world. This may induce Swedish speakers of English to believe that their proficiency is greater than it actually is. However, there are people who are aware of their shortcomings; a manager of a Swedish multinational company, when asked about their corporate language, answered, 'Bad English'.

When working as a lecturer in English for Business at Jönköping International Business School at Jönköping University, I showed my students how false friends can create an unintended obstacle in communication. Our discussions about the impact of such words often caused some amusement.

That said, in an international context, false friends are often no laughing matter.

I also meet linguistic false friends in my job as copyeditor of non-fiction texts, mainly doctoral dissertations and research papers for international journals, and I have been able to help numerous non-native writers of English avoid embarrassing mistakes.

Working as an interpreter has given me further insights into the problem of false friends. Speaking in a foreign language and listening to a foreign language easily leads to misunderstandings, especially when English is involved.

Introduction

The title of this book has been attributed to the Norwegian rally driver Petter Solberg, known for his unorthodox way of speaking English. However, it was coined by the talented comedian and impersonator Kristian Valen, who was poking fun at Solberg in a sketch, saying 'It's not the farts that kill—it's the smell'. I am grateful to Valen for giving me permission to use the phrase as the title of my book.

In Swedish, just as in Norwegian, **fart** means *speed* and **smäll** means *crash, bang,* or *impact.* Jokes about the word **fart** were, of course, prevalent long before Valen's skit. (**Skit** is another false friend. In English, it refers to *a short comedy sketch,* usually parodic. The Swedish word **skit** means *shit, crap, filth, turd,* etc.)

Solberg has also reportedly said, 'I came with a great fart and disappeared like a prick in the sky'. **Prick** means *dot* or *speck* in Norwegian as well as Swedish.

This book looks at hundreds of English words that have Swedish equivalents when it comes to spelling and/or pronunciation but not meaning. You will discover that common English words such as **and, art, bar, barn, be, blast, bra, chef, companion, concurrent, delicate, eventual, fan, faster, frisk, from, get, gift, glass, god, gymnasium, hamstring, hat, hem, hiss, husband, kiss, lager, mat, obligation, pant, plump, port, prat, prick, rapport, reclamation, reparation, semester, slut, spy, tax, visa, warehouse, worm, wrist,** and many, many others all have very different meanings from their Swedish counterparts. Additionally, you will learn where these tricky words come from and their original meanings.

Whether you do business in Sweden, are a translator, a language student, or just a language nerd interested in the history and use of words, this book will help you avoid making embarrassing or potentially disastrous mistakes when communicating in English or Swedish.

Each false friend is first presented in its English version, with an explanation in English and translation into Swedish and with its origin delineated. Then the similar-looking and/or similar-sounding Swedish word is explained and translated into English, and its origin is given.

What are false friends?

False friends are words in two languages that look and/or sound similar but whose meanings are completely or partially different. The two words may have (and often do have) the same origin.

The concept of false friends first appeared in a book by Kœssler and Derocquigny, *Les faux amis ou les trahisons du vocabulaire anglaise (Conseils aux Traducteures)* [False Friends, or the Treacheries of English Vocabulary. Advice to Translators] (Paris, 1928).

When it comes to words of the same origin, false friends are the result of semantic change, that is, the meaning of a word has changed over time. This may result in a broadening or narrowing of meaning or a completely different meaning. The word **adept** comes from Latin ADEPTUS meaning *who has achieved* (i.e., knowledge). In the Middle Ages, an adept was someone who alleged to have found the philosophers' stone, that is, who was a master in alchemy. In English, the adjective **adept** means *skilled at something*, and the noun **adept** means *a person who is skilled at something*. Surprisingly, even if the Swedish word **adept** has the same Latin origin as the English word, it has the opposite meaning of *pupil, disciple*, or *novice, beginner*.

A word in English may have one meaning and in other European languages another, even if the origin is the same. One example is **eventual**, which in English means *final, later, ultimate*. In other languages, such as Dutch, French, German, Italian, Spanish, and the Scandinavian languages, the meaning of **eventueel, éventuel, eventuell, eventuale, eventual**, and **eventuell** is *possible, potential* and the corresponding adverb *possibly, perhaps*. It is obvious that this may cause misunderstanding and even have serious consequences.

A word may originally have had two different meanings, and when the word came into another language, one meaning may have been lost. **Friend** corresponds to the archaic Swedish word **frände**, *relative*. The original Proto-Germanic word meant *someone whom one cares for*, which of course could refer to both friends and relatives. In English, the word lost its connotation with *relative*, and in the Scandinavian languages, it lost its reference to *friend*.

In addition to **false friends proper**, i.e., similar-looking words with completely different meanings, this book also includes **partial false friends**, words that look alike and have at least one meaning in common, but not all. **Present** in English is both a noun, an adjective, and a verb. As a noun, it means *a gift*; as an adjective, it means *current, existing, available, at hand*; and as a verb, it means *to give, to put forward, to introduce*. The Swedish word **present** is a noun only, meaning *a gift*. **Sax** in English is an abbreviation of **saxophone**. Swedish **sax** shares the same meaning, but in Swedish, **sax** also refers to **scissors**. A **fort** in both English and Swedish refers to a building erected to defend an area against attack, but in Swedish, **fort** also means *fast, rapidly*.

False cognates are words that look and/or sound alike but do not have the same origin. They may have the same or different meanings. Their similarity may be coincidental or a result of mutual influence. English **ask** (*inquire, question, request*) and Swedish **ask** (*ash-tree, small box*) are false cognates. The English word is of West Germanic origin; the Swedish one is from a Latin root.

This book deals with false friends in a wide meaning, including partial false friends, false cognates, and treacherous words in general.

... and what are treacherous words?

Treacherous words in this book are words or expressions that, although not false friends proper, may cause misunderstanding because of their similarity of form. This includes pseudo-English expressions in Swedish such as **after work, fit for fight**, and **happy end**, and misleading words such as **first floor** and **restroom**. Other words that have different connotations in English and Swedish are **backside, button up, city, house, must not, pack up, red day, speaker, spectacle, take place**, **villa**, and **way**.

Loanwords, words assimilated from one language into another, may take on a different meaning in the target language. One such English-Swedish example is **pocketbook**, another **hammock**.

Even symbols can be treacherous. In English, **the tick mark** ☑ means *correct* or *selected*; in Swedish it means the opposite, *wrong*. When you **cross out** something in English, ☒, you mark it as *wrong*; in Swedish the cross means *correct* or *selected*.

A note on Swedish forms of some English loanwords

The English verb **date**, *to go out with someone* that one is interested in romantically, is **dejta** in Swedish. Other verbs have undergone the same change, such as **strike**, which becomes **strejka**, **tape** is **tejpa**, **email** is **mejla**, **fight** is **fajtas**, **fake** is **fejka**, and **hype** is **hajpa**. Since the infinitive form of Swedish verbs often ends in **-a**, the Swedish versions of these English verbs avoid clumsy or misleading forms like **datea** or **data**.

Some English nouns are used in Swedish with their plural forms. A Swedish **bebis** is a **baby**. Again, inflection in Swedish looks better with the plural spelling. The plural form **bebisar** is better than **babyar** or **babyer**.

The headgear **cap** is **keps** in Swedish, and a **tip,** *information in a confidential manner,* is ett **tips**. Swedish **kex** comes from the plural of English **cake**, but it means *a biscuit*. In Swedish, the English plural form **muffins** is used also about a single **muffin**. And **clips** is used in Swedish about one **clip**. The English singular (railway) **rail** is **räls** in Swedish. The English plural **scarves** is sometimes used in Swedish for the singular **scarf**.

The plural form of an English word is also used by Swedes when they say **No comments** instead of the common English form **No comment**.

Periods in the history of languages

Indo-European began ca. 8100 years ago
Proto-Indo-European ca. 4500 to 2500 BC
Sanskrit began ca. 1500 BC
Proto-Germanic ca. 500 BC to 400 AD
West-Germanic ca. 200 to 800 AD
Latin began ca. 500 BC
Late Latin ca. 200 to 600
Vulgar Latin ca. 200 BC to 900 AD
Medieval Latin ca. 500 to 1500
Old Italian ca. 960 to the 1300s
Gothic ca. 200 to ca. 1560
Old Saxon ca. 700 to 1100
Old English (Anglo-Saxon) ca. 450 to 1150
Anglo-Norman ca. 1066 to 1300
Middle English ca. 1100 to 1500
Early Middle English ca. 1100 to 1250
Central Middle English ca. 1250 to 1400
Late Middle English ca. 1400 to 1500
Early Modern English ca. 1500 to 1700
Late Modern English ca. 1700 to the present
Middle Dutch ca. 1150 to 1500
Old French ca. 800 to 1350
Old High German ca. 750 to 1050
Middle High German ca. 1050 to 1350
Middle Low German ca. 1200 to 1650
Viking Age ca. 800 to 1050
Old Norse ca. 800 to 1350
Old West Norse ca. 800 to 1000
Old East Norse (Runic Swedish) ca. 800–1100
Old Swedish 1225 to 1526

The dates are indefinite. Naturally, it is difficult to state with certainty when a language began to be used and when it evolved into another language. Languages don't suddenly appear out of the blue; they grow from other languages, and they evolve into other languages. The transition is, of course, impossible to pinpoint.

The more specific dates for Old Swedish refer to the oldest manuscripts in Swedish, the law-rolls of the Swedish Provinces from 1225, and the year 1526, in which the New Testament was printed in Swedish.

Latin is considered a dead language, but it is the official language of Vatican City. Sanskrit is still alive today in India, mainly in religious and scholarly contexts.

Conventionally, in etymology, an asterisk (*) is used to show that a word or word form has been reconstructed by linguists using etymological inference since the word has not been found in any text.

English–Swedish false friends

A

accord

The English verb **accord**, Swedish **stämma överens**, means *to be consistent or harmonious*. It can also mean *to grant power or status* to someone, Swedish **bevilja**. The noun **accord** means *harmony, unity, concord*, Swedish **överensstämmelse**.

Accord comes from Latin AD, *to,* and COR, *heart*. In Old French, ACCORDER meant *to reconcile, be of one mind*. In Old English, the word was ACORDIAN. (The noun **accordion** comes from Italian ACCORDARE, *to tune.* Harmony, again.)

Of the same origin, the Swedish noun **ackord** is a musical term, *chord*. Another meaning of **ackord** is *contract, agreement*. **Ackordarbete** means *piecework*.

actual

While this English word means *real, existing, authentic,* etc., Swedish **aktuell** means *current, present, topical, up to date*. The Swedish nine o'clock news on TV is called **Aktuellt**.

Originally from Latin ACTUS, *act*, both the English and the Swedish word come from Old French ACTUEL, meaning *active, practical, now existing*. Obviously, Swedish settled for *now* and English for *existing*.

Actually in English is often used to express a contradictory opinion or to emphasize that something that was said is surprising.

adept

In English the adjective **adept** means *skilled at something*, Swedish **skicklig**, and the noun **adept** means a *person who is skilled at something*, Swedish **mästare**. The word comes from Latin ADEPTUS, meaning *who has achieved* (i.e., knowledge). In the Middle Ages, an **adept** was someone who alleged to have found the philosophers' stone, that is, who was *a master in alchemy*.

The Swedish noun **adept** means *pupil, disciple*, or *novice, beginner*. The word has the same Latin origin as the English **adept** and yet it has the opposite meaning.

adequate

In English this word means *satisfactory, sufficient, appropriate, acceptable*, etc., Swedish **tillräcklig, lämplig, lagom**, but in the early 1900s it began to imply *mediocre, just good enough, tolerable*, Swedish **medelmåttig**. From Latin ADAEQUATUS, *made equal to*, it came into English in the 1600s meaning *equal to what is needed or desired*.

The Swedish adjective **adekvat** has the same origin but usually means *apt, equivalent, exact, correct,* or *suitable.*

advocate

An **advocate** in English is *a spokesperson, representative,* or *champion,* someone who defends or supports a person or an idea, Swedish **förkämpe, försvarare**. As a verb it means *to publicly recommend or support,* Swedish **försvara, förorda, rekommendera**. The word comes from Latin ADVOCARE, which originally meant *to call to one's aid.*

The underlying meaning of assisting is reflected in the Swedish **advokat**, which is the equivalent of *lawyer, solicitor, barrister,* or *attorney.* In Scottish English, an **advocate** is *a barrister.*

affair

French À FAIRE means *to do*; modern French AFFAIRE means *business.* In the 1700s the word took on a meaning of *affair of the heart.* In English, **affair** can refer to *matters of business or of public interest* in addition to a sexual relationship.

Swedes can also **ha en affär**, have an extramarital sexual relationship; another colloquial verb is **vänsterprassla**. But if a Swede tells you, **'I have an affair'**, it might just as well be that he or she is a proud shop owner, since **affär** in Swedish usually means *shop* or *store,* in other words *a business.*

after-ski

This pseudo-English expression is mostly used in Scandinavia. In the Alps and generally in English, the French word **après-ski** is used. After-ski activities usually involve partying and music and may last late into night. Typically, there is no specific dress code.

after work

In Swedish, **after work** or **afterwork**, abbreviated **AW**, is also pseudo-English—it is an English expression but does not occur in English as a noun. In Sweden it refers to coworkers meeting for relaxation after work in a bar or restaurant, usually on a Friday, but AW can involve other collective activities such as karaoke, workout, ten-pin bowling, or a lecture.

The concept may have originated in London, where office employees met for a pint to relax after an intense day at work. Now, after-work activities are seen as an important part of team building in many parts of the world.

air

Air, Swedish **luft**, is *a mixture of mainly nitrogen and oxygen* that we breathe. The word comes from Latin AER via Old French AIR.

Air has several other meanings, such as *the space above the ground*, Swedish **luft**, or *appearance*, Swedish **utseende**. As a verb, it can mean *to* *broadcast* on radio or television, Swedish **sända**. You can **air** clothes, *hang them out* to make sure they are dry and fresh, Swedish **lufta, vädra**. You can also **air** a grievance, *express* it publicly, Swedish **uttrycka**. As a music term, **air** refers to *a tune* or *short song*, Swedish **melodi**, from Italian ARIA.

Är in Swedish is the present tense of the verb **vara**, *to be*. It corresponds to **am, are,** and **is** in English.

alley

The English word **alley** means *a narrow passageway* between or behind buildings, usually in older parts of towns or cities, Swedish **gränd**. The word comes from French ALLER, *to go*.

An **alley** can also be *a bowling alley*, a lane down which a bowling ball is rolled, Swedish **bowlingbana**.

The Swedish word **allé** has the same origin as **alley**, but it refers to *a street lined with trees*, in English an **avenue**. An **allé** can also be found in a park or cemetery.

a.m.

This abbreviation is used in English to denote *time before noon*. The Latin expression ANTE MERIDIEM means *before the middle of the day*. The abbreviation for *in the afternoon* is **p.m.** from Latin POST MERIDIEM. **Post** of course means *after*.

Swedes might mistake **a.m.** for **after midday**. In Swedish, **f.m.** is the abbreviation of **förmiddag**, *before noon*, and **e.m.** of **eftermiddag**, *afternoon*.

In Sweden, the 24-hour clock is generally used, which makes it unnecessary to specify whether you refer to a time in the morning or in the afternoon.

ambitious

If you are **ambitious**, you *have a strong desire to do or achieve something*. The word comes from Latin AMBITIOSUS, which meant *eager for public office*, from AMBIRE, *go around [canvassing votes]*.

In Swedish, **ambitiös** generally has the same meaning as the English word, but in English, **ambitious** can also have a negative meaning of *power-hungry, pushy, striving for fame, selfishly wanting the best*, Swedish **äregirig, ärelysten**. The Swedish word usually has a connotation of *conscientiousness* and *enterprising spirit*.

and

One of the most common words in English (according to the Oxford English Corpus, it is the fifth most common), **and** is a conjunction, a word to connect words or clauses. The corresponding Swedish word is **och**. **And** may originally have come from Proto-Indo-European *HÉNTI, *in front of, near, before*.

A Swedish **and** is *a wild duck* or *mallard*, Latin *Anas platyrhynchos*.

anger

The Middle English word ANGER meant *grief, affliction, pain, trouble, sorrow*. The word comes from Old Norse ANGR, *grief*.

In modern English, **anger** means *wrath, rage, a strong feeling of being upset or annoyed because of something wrong or bad*, or, according to Merriam-Webster, *'an intense emotional state induced by displeasure'*. The word is, of course, related to **angry**. The Swedish equivalent to **anger** is **ilska, vrede**.

The Swedish word **ånger** means *remorse* or *regret*. It is related to the Latin word ANGOR, *suffocation, difficulty in breathing*.

In northern Sweden there are place names such as **Lövånger** or **Njutånger**. This ending **-ånger** comes from another Old Norse ANGR meaning *bay, rounded fjord*, originally from a Proto-Germanic word meaning *meadow, lowland*.

In England, in Lancashire and Northumberland, for example, there are a few places called **Angerton** with the same meaning of *bay* or *lowland*. TUN in Old English meant *enclosure, farmstead*, or *village*.

In Swedish, **anger** (with a different pronunciation from the English) is the present tense of the verb **ange**, which means *indicate, turn in, denounce, point out [especially somebody to the police]*.

announce

When you **announce** something, you *make it publicly known*. The Latin word ADNUNTIARE means *declare*. It comes from Latin NUNTIUS, *messenger*. The Swedish word for **announce** is **meddela, tillkännage**.

Annonsera in Swedish means that you pay to make something known. In other words, you *advertise*.

apart

In English, if people or things are **apart**, they are *separated* in time or space, Swedish **fristående, isär, åtskilda**. And if things **fall apart**, they are *in a very bad condition*. **Apart from** is the same as *except for*, Swedish **bortsett från, utom**.

Apart comes from Latin AD-, *to*, and PARTEM, *part, piece*.

With the same Latin origin, **apart** in Swedish means *eccentric, odd*.

archives

Archives is a word that can be used in the singular or the plural, and it is grammatically correct to say **an archives**. The word refers to *a collection of documents, records, or other primary sources of historical interest* as well as *the place where they are stored* and *the organization that collects and maintains the materials*. **Archive** can also be used as a verb, meaning *to store something in an archives*. A person in charge of an archives is an **archivist**.

Arkiv in Swedish has a broader meaning, including also more recent documents and where they are stored. In English such documents are called **files** or **records** or, if they are about individual persons, **dossiers**. They are stored in a **filing cabinet** or a **filing room**. The person who manages an archives is **arkivarie** in Swedish.

The English and the Swedish word have the same origin, a Greek word ARCHEIA meaning *public records*, from ARCHE, *government*.

argument

In English, the noun **argument** has two meanings, *quarrel, disagreement, dispute*, Swedish **gräl**, and *reasoning, logic, justification*, Swedish **resonemang, slutledning**.

Argument in Swedish means *statement, reason, cause, proof*.

From the Latin word ARGUER, meaning *to make clear, prove, accuse*, Middle English ARGUMENT referred to *the process of reasoning*.

ark

Noah's **ark**, according to the Bible, was *a ship* built by Noah to save him and his family and two of every kind of animal from the Flood.

The Ark of the Covenant is *a cupboard or chest* in which the Torah scrolls are kept in a synagogue.

The English **ark** comes from Latin ARCA, *large box, chest*.

The Swedish **ark** shares those two meanings with English, **Noaks ark** and **förbundsarken**, respectively, but more commonly, **ark** means *a sheet of paper*. August Strindberg, one of Sweden's most celebrated authors, wrote a short story called **Ett halvt ark papper**, *Half a Sheet of Foolscap*, in which the story of two years in a man's life is told through a list of telephone numbers, the first one being his fiancée's and the last the undertaker's. Strindberg's story has been translated into almost forty languages.

Swedish **ark** comes from Latin ARCUS, *bow, arch*, which refers to a bent or folded piece of parchment.

arm

Arm in English is *a part of your body*, Swedish **arm**. We have got two, with hands at each end. The word comes from Sanskrit ÎRMA, *arm, shoulder, foreleg*. **Arms** means *weapons*, Swedish **vapen**, and you can **arm** somebody, *provide them with weapons*, Swedish **beväpna**. You can also **arm** yourself with information or facts, etc., to be prepared for an argument or a tricky situation. **Arms** in the meaning of *weapons* comes from Latin ARMA, *tools of war*.

A **coat of arms,** Swedish **vapensköld,** is *a shield* with patterns or images as a symbol of a noble family, a town, or a university. The word **arms** is also used in names of pubs or taverns, such as **The King's Arms**.

In Swedish, **arm**, plural **armar**, refers to *the body part*. **Arm** is also an adjective in Swedish, meaning *poor* or *wretched*. This meaning is shared with some dialects in the UK, particularly in Scotland. In Old English EARM meant *poor* or *wretched*.

art

Art originally meant *skill as a result of learning or practice*. Boxing used to be called *the noble art of self-defence*. In Middle English the word took on the sense of *skill in scholarship and learning,* which lives on in the university degrees **Bachelor of Arts** and **Master of Arts**. The meaning of *skill in creative arts*, especially painting, sculpture, etc., appeared in the 1600s. **Art** comes from Latin ARS, *art*.

Art is also an old English verb form, the present tense of **be** in the second person singular, **thou art**, *you are*.

English **art** is **konst** in Swedish, from a German word meaning *to know*, and the Swedish word **art** means *species, sort*. Its origin may be in an Old High German word for *ploughing*, which then developed into *field* and *domicile,* leading to *origin, nature, character*.

artist

An **artist** is *someone who paints, draws, or makes sculptures*, that is, *creates fine art*. The word comes from medieval Latin ARTISTA, from Latin ARS, *art*. The corresponding Swedish word is **konstnär**.

In English, **artist** can also refer to *an artiste, performer,* or *entertainer*, such as a musician, an actor, a dancer, or other performer. This is also what the Swedish word **artist** means. However, **artist** in Swedish does not have the connotation with fine art.

ask

In English you can **ask a question**, Swedish **fråga**, or **ask somebody to do something for you**, Swedish **be**. You can also **ask a person to dinner or to dance**, Swedish **bjuda**. **Ask** comes from a Proto-Indo-European word meaning *to wish* or *request*, in Old English ASCIAN.

In Swedish, **ask** (from another Proto-Indo-European word meaning *ash*) is either *an ash-tree, Fraxinus excelsior,* or *a small box*, usually with a loose lid.

English **ask** and Swedish **ask** are false cognates; they look the same but do not have the same origin.

aspect

From Latin ASPICERE, *look at*, **aspect** in Middle English meant *[a way of] looking*. Now the word has mainly two meanings, *characteristic, feature,* Swedish **utseende**, and *outlook, view, situation,* or *position*, Swedish **läge**. **Aspect** is also a technical term; it means *the ratio of height to width* of, for example, a TV screen. Planets have **aspects**, *the angles that planets make to each other*, and verbs have **aspects**, telling us *whether an action is ongoing or completed. The direction* in which a building or window faces is its **aspect**.

Swedish **aspekt** means *point of view, perspective, consideration*, but it shares the technical, astronomical, and linguistic meanings with English **aspect**.

axe

An **axe** (American English **ax**) is a *tool* for chopping wood. The word is also a verb meaning *to cut* or, figuratively, *suddenly cancel or dismiss*. It is of Germanic origin, in Old English ÆX. The noun **axe** is **yxa** in Swedish.

Ax in Swedish refers to *the spike* of a plant or *the ear* of corn. The word comes from Proto-Germanic *AHAZ or *AHIZ. **Ax** is also *the part of a key* that you put into a lock.

axel

The word **axel** is used in English (and many other languages, including Swedish) to denote *a jump in figure skating,* considered the most difficult jump. It was named after the Norwegian figure skater Axel Paulsen, who created the jump in 1882.

In Swedish, **Axel** is also *a boy's name* (I have a grandson called Axel). The name is a Nordic version of the biblical name ABSALON or ABSALOM, in Hebrew AVSHALOM, meaning *my father is peace.*

The Swedish noun **axel** means *axis, axle,* related to Latin AXIS, or *shoulder,* from Old Norse OXL and Old Swedish AXL.

B

back

Back is the opposite of **front**. You can carry a rucksack on your **back**, Swedish **rygg**, or scribble something on the **back**, Swedish **baksida**, of an envelope.

You can also **go back**, *return* to a place, Swedish **återvända**.

The verb **back** means *to support, to be in favour of,* Swedish **stödja**, or *to walk or drive backwards,* Swedish **backa**.

In sports such as football or ice hockey, a **back** is *a defender*. The corresponding Swedish word is also **back**.

A **back street** is *away from the main streets*, Swedish **bakgata**, and a **back copy** or **back issue** of a magazine is *an old copy*, Swedish **gammalt nummer** or **äldre nummer**.

With a Germanic origin, possibly from Proto-Indo-European *b^heg-*, *to bend*, **back** was BÆC in Old English; it is related to Swedish and Norwegian BAK.

Back in Swedish has three definitions: *a crate* or *tray, a reverse gear*, and, just as in English, *a defender* in games such as football, ice hockey, etc.

The Swedish word **backe** means *hill* or *slope*. It can also refer to *the ground*.

backside

Your **backside** in English is what you sit on, your *posterior*, your *behind*, your *rump, butt*, or *bottom*. The Swedish equivalent is **bak** or **rumpa**.

The Swedish **baksida** is *the back* of, for example, a book or a building, or *the reverse* of a coin. **Medaljens baksida** is *the reverse side of the medal*.

bad

In Middle English, BAD or BADDE meant *wicked* or *evil*, Swedish **dålig, elak**. It still has this meaning in modern English together with *not good, unfavourable, not suitable, unhealthy, false*, etc.

Foreign tourists in Sweden may wonder why there are so many bad hotels. **Bad** is in Swedish *bath*, and a **badhotell** is quite simply *a spa hotel* or *seaside hotel*; they are usually not bad at all. **Bad** comes from a Germanic root in the sense of *dab, heat with a compress*. It is, of course related to English **bath**.

Bad in Swedish is also the past tense of **be** (archaic **bedja**), *prayed* or *asked*, possibly from an Indo-European root *BHEDH, *press*.

The Swedish verb **badda** means *dab*.

See also **be**.

balk

The English verb **balk** means *to hinder* or *thwart* a person or a plan or *to prevent* somebody from having something, Swedish **hindra**. If you **balk at** something, you are *hesitant or unwilling* to accept it, Swedish **dra sig för, undvika**.

The noun **balk** refers to *a rough timber beam*, Swedish **balk** or **bjälke**. **Balk** comes from Old Norse BÁLKR, *partition, unploughed ridge*. In Middle English the word took on the meaning of *obstacle*, giving rise to the meanings *hesitate* and *hinder*.

In Swedish, **balk** is a wooden *beam* or a metal *girder*. In law language, **balk** is *a legal code* or *a main section* of Swedish law.

bar

Bar is a word with many meanings in both English and Swedish, but it is only *the place where you can buy drinks* that is common to the two languages. The original English word came from the French BARRE in the late 1200s and meant *a rod of iron used to fasten a door or gate*. In the 1500s it developed into referring to *anything that obstructs or hinders*. The verb **bar** means *to prevent* or *forbid*, Swedish **[för]hindra, förbjuda**. **A bar of soap**, Swedish **tvål**, got its name from the similarity to a rod. The **bar** where you buy drinks has its name from the barrier or counter where drinks are served.

More modern expressions are **bar graph**, used to visualize statistics, Swedish **stapeldiagram**, and **barcode** or **bar code**, a pattern of parallel lines of varying widths used for stock control, Swedish **streckkod**. And if you are **behind bars**, you are in prison, Swedish **bakom galler**. The preposition **bar** means *apart from, except*, Swedish **utom**.

If you are **called to the Bar**, you are not invited to the counter to have a drink. The expression means that you can work as a **barrister**, *a lawyer who can argue in court on behalf of somebody*. This **bar** refers to *a partition* in a courtroom, behind which an accused person stands, Swedish **skrank**.

In Sweden in the 1950s, **bar** or **mjölkbar** (**milk bar**) referred to a type of *simpler restaurant* with self-service. Nowadays, just as in English, **bar** generally means a drinking place, but it has other meanings that are different from English. One is *naked, nude,* or *bare*. **Bar** is also the past tense of the verb **bära,** *carried* or *wore*.

barn

BERERN in Old English came from BERE, *barley* and ERN or ÆRN, *house*. In other words, a **barn** was *a house for barley*. Nowadays we store hay or all sorts of grain there. The Swedish word is **lada** or **loge**.

Barn in Swedish means *child* or *children* (the singular and plural forms are the same). The word is related to the verb **bära,** *bear* or *carry*. In English, you say that a child is **born**. In Scotland and Northern England, **bairn** is a word for *child*. Before 1700 it was used generally as an English word for *child*.

be

The English verb **be**, from Old English BEON, means *to exist* or *occur, to represent or consist of*, Swedish **vara**. The conjugated forms **am** and **is** on the one hand and **was** and **were** on the other come from different Indo-European roots. The origin of **are** is uncertain.

The Swedish verb **be** means *to pray* or *ask*. It comes from Gothic BIDJAN and is related to English **bid**. The Old Swedish form was BEDHIA.

See also **bad**.

become

The English verb **become** means *to begin to be, develop into*, Swedish **bli**, or (about clothes) *to suit, look good on*, Swedish **passa, klä**. Old English BECUMAN, of Germanic origin, meant *to come to a place, come to be or do something*.

Bekomma in Swedish means *to have effect on* or *to bother*. **Det bekommer mig ingenting** is in English **I think nothing of it**.

beef

The English word **beef**, *meat from cattle*, Swedish **nötkött** or **oxkött**, comes from Latin BOS, *ox*, via French BOEF. In English slang, it can also mean *muscle, strength*, or, especially in North American slang, *complaint, criticism, grievance, objection*, etc.

In Swedish, **biff** means *steak*, and the Swedish word **stek** means *roast*. **Pannbiff** is in English *Salisbury steak*.

befall

Befall is used to indicate that something (usually bad) *happens* to a person, Swedish **hända, drabba**. The word comes from Old English BEFEALLAN, *to fall*, from Proto-Germanic *BIFALLANA, equivalent to *be-* and *fall*.

Befalla in Swedish means *to order* or *command*. The word is related to Anglo-Saxon BEFEOLAN, *to deliver, entrust*.

beholder

Beholder is an archaic word in English referring to a *person who observes somebody or something*, Swedish **betraktare, åskådare**. The verb **behold** comes from Old English BI-, *thoroughly*, and HALDAN, *to hold*. In other Germanic languages, corresponding words have the meaning of *maintain* or *retain*. The notion of *observing* is known only in English.

Behållare in Swedish, of the same Old English origin, is *a container* or *receptacle*. It retains the Germanic sense of the word.

beware

Beware means *to be cautious, be on your guard, look out* in English. It comes from Middle English BEN WARE, *to be ware, be on one's guard*. The corresponding Swedish phrase is **akta sig, se upp**.

The Swedish word **bevara** means *to preserve, keep, maintain*. It comes from a Proto-Germanic word that was a combination of *be* and *last*.

billion

An English **billion** is *one thousand million*, which in Swedish (and in other European languages) is a **miljard**. **Miljard** comes from Latin MILLE, *thousand*, plus the French ending -ARD. It is written as a one followed by nine noughts or 10^9.

A Swedish **biljon** is a lot more, *one million million*, in English a **trillion**. It is written as a one followed by twelve noughts or 10^{12}.

Million and **billion** also come from Latin MILLE, *thousand*. **Bi-** is from Latin BIS, meaning *twice*.

When a Swedish journalist mentions **biljon** in an article, there is a great chance that some readers, well aware of the difference in meaning between English **billion** and Swedish **biljon**, will write and ask, 'Don't you mean **miljard**?' They suspect that the journalist has copied the article from an English original without knowing the difference.

black

Black is of course a colour, or to be exact, *the absence of colour*, Swedish **svart**. The word comes from Old English BLÆK, *black, dark,* and *ink*.

To be **in the black** means *to be financially solvent or profitable*. The opposite, be **in the red**, means that you owe more money than you earn, you *make a loss*. These two expressions supposedly come from the habit of using red ink to denote a loss or deficit in bookkeeping.

The Swedish word **bläck**, *ink*, is related to **black**. In Swedish, there is also the word **black**. **En black om foten** denotes an *obstacle* or *impediment*, something that is a burden or hindrance. A **black** was a lump of wood or iron tied to the foot of a horse or a prisoner to stop them from escaping. The word is possibly related to **block**.

In Swedish slang, if you are **black**, you are *broke, without money*; in other words, you are *in the red*.

blank

Leave this page blank means that you must leave it *empty*, Swedish **tom**. The word comes from Old French BLANC, meaning *white*. A **blank** is also *an empty space* between words or lines on, for example, a computer screen, Swedish **mellanrum**. And you can have **a blank look**, *showing no expression*, Swedish **tom blick**.

The Swedish word **blank** has the same origin, but it means *shiny*. If something is white, it is also *bright* and *shining*.

blanket

A **blanket** is *a large piece of woollen or similar material* used to cover a bed or to wrap around you for warmth. The Swedish word is **filt**. Of Germanic origin, **blanket** comes from Old French BLANC, *white*.

The Swedish word **blankett** means *a paper form to fill in or complete*. The word comes from French BLANQUET, which also derives from BLANC, *white*, in other words, *a white paper*.

blast

The noun **blast** means *an explosion*, Swedish **explosion**, *a sudden strong blow of air*, Swedish **tryckvåg**, or *a sudden loud noise*, Swedish **oljud**. In colloquial Northern American English, it also means *a very enjoyable experience*.

As a verb, **blast** means *to destroy something by using explosives*, Swedish **spränga, förstöra**, *to be very loud*, Swedish **dåna**, or *to criticize strongly*, Swedish **skälla ut**.

Blast! is also used as an *exclamation* to express annoyance, Swedish **jäklar!** or **tusan!**

Blast is of Germanic origin, in Old English BLÆST. It is related to **blaze**.

In Swedish, **blast** is used in botany in the sense of *tops* or *haulm*, leaves and stems of root vegetables. The word is possibly related to BLAD, *leaf*.

bleak

The adjective **bleak** is often used about the weather or about a place. It means *cold, not welcoming, gloomy, dreary*, in Swedish **kylig, kulen, dyster, trist**. **Bleak** is of Germanic origin, in Old English BLAC and in Old Norse BLEIKR, both meaning *shining, white*, related to **bleach**.

The Swedish adjective **blek** means *pale* or *faint*. It has the same origin as **bleak**.

blot

A **blot** is *a stain or spot* that makes something dirty, Swedish **fläck**. If you **blot your copybook**, you do something that *spoils the opinion that people have about you*. You can also **blot** a wet surface by *pressing a cloth* on it to dry it, Swedish **torka upp**. The origin of the word is unclear, possibly from Old Norse BLETTR, *spot, stain*.

Blot in Swedish (pronounced with a long **o** as in **too**) was an ancient heathen Old Norse *sacrificial ceremony*. The word is related to Gothic BLÔTAN, *to worship*, perhaps originally *to worship with incantation and sacrifice*.

The Swedish word **blott** is pronounced like English **blot**. It means *only, but, merely*; it is now old-fashioned or, as linguists would say, archaic. It is also used in phrases such as **blotta tanken**, *the very thought*. **Blott** comes from Middle Low German BLÔT from Proto-Germanic *BLAUTAZ.

Blått with the same pronunciation is an inflection of **blå**, *blue*.

Swedish **blöt** means *wet* or *soggy*. The word is related to **blott**, but also to Latin FLUIDUS, *fluid, liquid*.

board

A **board** in English is *a long flat piece of wood* used for making walls, floors, etc., Swedish **bräda**. It is also *a flat surface on a wall* used to write on or show information on, Swedish **anslagstavla**. You can chop vegetables or play chess and other games on a **board**, Swedish **bräda** and **bräde**, respectively. A **board** is also *a group of people in an organization* who make decisions, in Swedish **styrelse**. As a verb, **board** means *to get on a bus, train, plane, etc.*, to travel somewhere, Swedish **borda, stiga på**. The word is of Germanic origin, in Old English BORD.

Of the same origin, **bord** in Swedish means *table* as well as *plank*. The Swedish word **bård** means *edging* or *fringe*.

bone

The Swedish word **ben** has two meanings. One is the same as the English **bone**, meaning a part of *what constitutes the skeleton* of a person or an animal.

The other meaning of the Swedish word **ben** is *leg* in the sense of what you use when you walk. **Ben** also refers to the (usually four) *legs of a table or a chair*.

Bone and **ben** have the same Proto-Germanic origin meaning *straight*.

The two meanings of **ben** in Swedish are reflected in a pun that is unintelligible in English: **Röntgen är något konstigt: man fotograferar armarna och ser benen**. *X-ray is a strange thing. You photograph the arms and see the legs/the bones.*

boot

A **boot**, Swedish **känga**, is a type of sturdy *footwear*, usually made of leather. **Wellington boots** or **Wellingtons**, Swedish **stövlar**, are made of rubber and are waterproof. **Boot** comes from Old French BOTE.

In UK English, a **boot** is also *a space at the back of a car* for luggage, Swedish **bagagelucka**. In North American English this is called a **trunk**.

As a verb, **boot** means *to kick hard*, Swedish **sparka**. A more modern sense of the word is *to start a computer*, from **bootstrap**, *a collection of bits of data code*. The original meaning of **bootstrap** was a small *loop of leather* at the back of a boot used to pull on the boot. Now **bootstrap** is used also in business language in the sense of starting with existing resources with the aim of creating something bigger, such as *the start-up of a company with very little capital*.

The adverb **to boot** means *as well, in addition*, Swedish **dessutom, till på köpet**.

The Swedish word **bot** with the same pronunciation as **boot** means *remedy* or *cure, penance,* and a *fine*. Like the English **boot**, it is related to Old Saxon BOTA.

borrow

Old English **BORGIAN** meant *borrow against security.* **Borgen** in Swedish means *bail, security.*

You should not be surprised if a Swede asks to **borrow your bathroom**. You need not worry that your bathroom will be carried away to be returned later. The Swedish word for **borrow** is **låna,** which is often used in the sense of *use.* But many Swedes don't know that they should say **May I use your bathroom?**

bot

Bot (from **ROBOT**), Swedish **bot,** is *a computer program* created to carry out automatic operations, often with the help of artificial intelligence.

A **bot** is also *the larva of the botfly,* which is a parasite affecting horses, Swedish **styngfluga**. The word is probably of Low German origin.

For the Swedish word **bot**, see **Boot**.

boutique

Boutique in English is *a small shop* that sells fashionable clothes and accessories. The word can also refer to any small business that is fashionable and sophisticated. This word with its original French spelling is also used in Swedish with the same meaning.

Butik in Swedish is just any *small shop,* fashionable or not.

Boutique and **butik** come from Greek APOTHEKE and Latin APOTHECA via French BOUTIQUE. **Apotek** in Swedish is *a pharmacy* or *chemist's*.

bra

The English noun **bra** comes from French BRASSIÈRE and means *an undergarment used to support and cover breasts.* The Swedish word for this is **bysthållare** (literally *bust holder*), abbreviated **BH**, but often also written **behå**.

The Swedish word **bra** means *good.* It comes from German BRAV and French BRAVE (compare Italian **bravo**).

branch

Branch means *a part of a tree* that grows out from a trunk or bough, Swedish **gren**. It can also refer to *an extension* of a railway or underground line or a river. Another meaning is *a subsidiary or division of a large business* operating locally, Swedish **filial**. The word can also be used as a verb.

Bransch in Swedish means *industry, trade, line of business.* The English and the Swedish word have the same French origin, BRANCHE, meaning *branch* of a tree, from late Latin BRANCA, *footprint* or *paw.*

brand

A **brand** is a name or trademark that distinguishes a product from others, Swedish **varumärke**. In Old English, BRAND meant *burning*, from a Proto-Germanic word meaning *flame*. To identify livestock, a red-hot iron is used; this kind of **branding**, Swedish **brännmärkning**, is now forbidden in Sweden. **Branding** in present-day English has come to mean the process of *creating an identity* for a business in order to promote it and its products or service. A **brand-new car** is *a completely new car*.

In Swedish, **brand** is also related to burning. It means *fire* or *conflagration*, but the word is also used to mean *gangrene*, death of body tissue, and *blight* or *rust*, a plant disease.

brief

Brief is an adjective meaning *continuing for a short time* or *using very few words*, Swedish **kort**. It can also mean *[to give somebody] instructions or information about a job or a task*. Swedish has kept the verb but added an ending, **briefa**. A **brief** is also *a summary of facts* in a court case, Swedish **sammandrag**.

Briefs are men's or women's *underwear* on the lower part of the body, Swedish **trosor, kalsonger**.

Brief comes from Latin BREVIS, *short*.

Brev in Swedish has the same Latin origin, but it means *letter* in the sense of note, communication.

building society

Swedes would misunderstand this to mean **byggföretag,** *construction company.* A **building society** in the UK (and a **savings and loan association** in the USA and Australia) is *a financial organization that lends its members money to buy (or renovate) a house and pays interest on investments.*

The Swedish translation of **building society** is *bolåneinstitut.*

bull

A **bull** is *the male of domestic cattle* or other animals such as the elephant or the whale, Swedish **tjur**. The word **bull** signifies something strong or clumsy. **A bull in a china shop** is someone who is very *clumsy,* Swedish **en elefant i en porslinsbutik**. Bull comes from Old Norse BOLI.

A **bull market,** Swedish **hausse,** is when *the price of shares on a stock market is going up* (the opposite is a **bear market**). **Bull** can also mean *nonsense,* Swedish **skitprat**.

The **bull's eye**, Swedish **prick**, is *the centre of a target,* especially in the game of darts.

A **papal bull**, Swedish **påvebulla**, is an official letter or document from the Pope. A BULLA was *the leaden seal* affixed to such documents. (Originally the bulla was a small round box to protect the seal.)

The Swedish word **bulle** means *bun* or *roll*. **Köttbulle** is *a meatball*. **Bulle** comes from a Proto-Germanic word meaning *round object*. It is related to English **ball** and **bowl**.

In Stockholm slang, **bulle** means *taxi* or *cab*.

bus

The English word **bus** and the Swedish **buss** both come from Latin OMNIBUS, *for all, for everybody*.

In Sweden **buss** refers to both **bus** (for public transport) and **coach** (usually chartered for long-distance travel).

Bus in Swedish means *practical joke, mischief, pranks*, or *tricks*. The verb **busa** comes from Middle Low German BUSEN, *live in flair and extravagance*.

butter

Butter probably came from the Greek word BOUTURON, *cow-cheese*. It came via Latin into Old English BUTERE, *the fatty part of milk*. The Swedish word is **smör**.

Butter in Swedish has a completely different etymology and meaning. From Low German BUTT, *coarse, rough, rude, clumsy*, it means *sullen, sulky, morose, grumpy*.

button up

When you **button up**, you *close your shirt, jacket, etc.* The opposite, *to open a jacket, etc.*, is **unbutton**.

In Swedish, it's the other way around. Att **knäppa upp** means to **unbutton**. Button up is in Swedish **knäppa** or **knäppa igen**.

This is the same as with **pack up** and **unpack**. Swedish **packa upp** is **unpack**.

See also **pack up**.

by

The English preposition **by** means *through the agency of* or *via, by way of*, Swedish **av, genom**. It can also mean *near, next to,* or *close to*, Swedish **vid**. **By** can also indicate a deadline: **Send me the report by Friday**, Swedish **senast**. The word is of Germanic origin and was BI or BE in Old English.

In Swedish, **by** is a noun meaning *village*. The word comes from Old Norse BYR or BØR, *homestead, town*, related to **bo**, *live, dwell*. **By** can also mean *a gust*, a sudden strong rush of wind.

C

cabinet

In English, a **cabinet** is *a cupboard* for storing or displaying things, Swedish **skåp**. The word also refers to *a group of senior ministers in a government*. Another meaning of **cabinet** is *a TV, radio, or loudspeaker enclosure*, Swedish **TV-skåp, radioskåp, högtalarlåda**. The word comes from 16th century English CABIN plus the diminutive ending -ET, influenced by French CABINET.

Kabinett in Swedish means *chamber, small room*, but it shares the reference to *a part of a government* with English. **Kabinett** is also an archaic word for *toilet, lavatory*.

canine

Canine, from Latin CANIS, *dog*, Swedish **hund**, is an adjective meaning *related to dogs*. The noun **canine** refers to a pointed *tooth*, Swedish **hörntand**.

The Swedish noun **kanin** means *rabbit*. It comes from Latin CUNICULUS, *rabbit*.

camp

From Latin CAMPUS, *level ground*, **camp** means *a place with tents or huts for temporary accommodation*, usually for soldiers, travellers, or refugees. **Camp** is also a summer holiday programme for children. Figuratively, **camp** refers to *the supporters* of, for example, a political party. English **camp** is **läger** in Swedish. **Camp** is also used as a verb meaning *to spend part of a holiday in a tent, etc.*, Swedish **campa** or **kampa**.

Another **camp** is used in contemporary popular culture. It comes from French SE CAMPER, *to strike a pose, behave provocatively*, and is used as an adjective, *exaggerated, affected*, a noun, *exaggerated behaviour*, and a verb, *to behave in a theatrical way*. The word was brought into general discussion through *Notes on 'Camp'*, an essay by the American writer, philosopher, and critic Susan Sontag in 1964. It is (or was) used in Swedish, too.

In Swedish, **kamp** means *fight, battle, struggle*. In Old Saxon, KAMP meant *an enclosed area for a duel* or simply *a duel*. **Kamp** in Swedish also used to denote *a war-horse* or *a jade*, a broken-down, worthless horse. The origin of the word is unknown, but the Norwegian word GAMP means *big sturdy body or horse*.

car

A **car** is *an automobile*, a road vehicle, Swedish **bil**. Especially in North American English, a **car** is also *a part of a train*, Swedish **vagn**.

Car comes from Latin **carrum, carrus**, *vehicle*.

In Swedish, **kar** means *tub* or *vat*. It comes from Old Swedish KAR, *chest, box*. With the same pronunciation, **karl** means *man* and, in colloquial language, *bloke, fellow*, or *chap*. **Karl** is related to Old English CEORL, *husband, farmer*. It is also a Swedish name, related to **Charles**.

cast

Cast comes from Old Norse KASTA, *to cast* or *throw*, **kasta** in Swedish. This verb is used with several meanings in English, usually figuratively. The sun can **cast its light,** Swedish **kasta ljus,** (or **a shadow**, Swedish **skugga**) on a landscape; you can **cast an eye**, Swedish **kasta ett öga,** on something; you can **cast your vote**, Swedish **avge sin röst**, in an election; you can **cast light**, Swedish **kasta ljus**, on a problem. Someone can **cast doubt** on something they have heard, Swedish **ifrågasätta**. A criminal may be **cast into prison**, Swedish **kastas i fängelse**, and a ship can **cast anchor**, Swedish **kasta ankare**. **Casting** (the same in Swedish) is a type of sport fishing. To **cast** is also *to pour molten metal into a mould* to create, for example, a church bell, Swedish **gjuta**. *To select actors* for a film or a play is **casting**, Swedish **rollbesättning**.

The noun **cast** can refer to *an object made by pouring molten metal into a mould* or *the mould* itself, Swedish **avgjutning**. It can also be *a bandage stiffened by plaster* to support a broken limb, Swedish **gipsförband**. The actors in a film or play constitute the **cast**, Swedish **ensemble**.

Kast in Swedish is *a throw*. **Kast** was also used to denote *the case* in which the types (the letters and signs) were kept in a printing office (this was before computers took over printing). Capital letters were kept in an upper case and small letters in a lower case, which is how *uppercase and lowercase letters* got their names in English.

Swedish **kast** also corresponds to English **caste**, referring to *a hereditary class* in Hindu society or to any group of people who inherit privileges. The word comes from Latin CASTUS, *chaste*.

The Swedish verb **kasta** is **throw** in English but, as you can see above, it has many collocations in common with English *cast*.

cavalier

As a noun, **Cavalier** refers to *a supporter of the King* against Parliament in the English Civil War in the 17th century (the opponents were called Roundheads). The word comes from Latin CABALLARIUS, *horseman*. A **cavalier** was also *an attractive and attentive man* acting as a lady's escort.

The adjective **cavalier** means *not caring about other people's feelings, haughty, arrogant, indifferent, etc.*, Swedish **överlägsen, nonchalant**.

In Swedish, **kavaljer** means *a gentleman, a beau*, or *a dinner partner or dance partner*.

chef

The English **chef** is *the chief cook* in a restaurant, Swedish **köksmästare** (literally *kitchen master*). In French, a **chef de cuisine** is *the head of the kitchen*. **Chef** comes from Latin CAPUT, *head*.

In Swedish, the word **chef** has a more general meaning of *employer* or *boss*, which, as we have seen, the original Latin word also had.

chemist

A **chemist's** (a chemist's shop) in the UK is *a pharmacy*, a place where you can buy medical drugs and medicines as well as toiletries, cosmetics, etc. In Sweden, the shop where you buy medicine is **apotek**. (See also **boutique** above.)

A **chemist** is also *a person who studies chemistry or carries out research in chemistry*.

Kemist in Swedish only refers to the person mentioned above, not the shop.

Chemistry and **kemi** come from Greek KHEMEIA or KHYMEIA, *mixture*.

chips

A **chip** is *a splinter or fragment* resulting from chopping or cutting wood or stone, Swedish **flisa, spån**. **Chips** are also long rectangular pieces of deep-fried potato, Swedish **pommes frites** (which is a French loanword). A **microchip** is used in an integrated circuit in computers. **Chip** is related to Old English FORCIPPIAN, *to cut off*.

Chips in Swedish are what the English call *crisps*, thin slices of potato made crisp by being fried.

citation

Citation in English has several meanings. From Latin CITARE, *to summon, call*, it has the meaning of *summons*, Swedish **kallelse**. The word can also mean *quotation*, Swedish **citat**, a piece of text that you have borrowed from another writer and need to indicate with the help of citation marks or quotation marks. Another meaning of **citation** is *award, commendation, tribute*, or *honourable mention*, Swedish **hedersomnämnande**.

In Swedish, **citation** (or, more often, **citat**) only means *quotation*.

city

In English, a **city** is *an inhabited place that is larger or more important than a town*. Cities are often surrounded by suburbs. In the UK, a large town that is *the seat of a bishop*, that is, has a cathedral, is also called a **city**. In Swedish, both **city** and **town** are called **stad**. **City** comes via Old French from Latin CIVIS, *citizen*.

Greater London comprises two cities, the City of London and the City of Westminster, and 32 boroughs (Lambeth, Southwark, Islington, Camden, Ealing, Greenwich, Croydon, Harrow, to mention a few). When mass media talk about **the City**, they refer to the financial centre of the UK with the Stock Exchange and banks, and **Westminster** represents Parliament and the government.

In Sweden, the word **city** refers to *a city centre*, particularly in Stockholm. In North American English the corresponding word is **downtown**, the commercial area of a city.

civil engineer

The origin of the English **engineer** and the Swedish **ingenjör** is a French word, INGENIÉUR, meaning *builder of war machines*.

A **civil engineer** designs and maintains roads, bridges, etc. In Swedish, this corresponds to a **väg- och vattenbyggnadsingenjör**, *a road and water construction engineer*.

The Swedish title **civilingenjör** indicates that the bearer has *a Master of Science in Engineering*.

clap

Clap in English is a verb. You can **clap your hands**, Swedish **klappa händerna**, to show *appreciation*, for instance at the theatre or a concert. **Clap** also means *to slap someone on the back or shoulder*. You can also **clap a door shut** or even **clap somebody into prison**. Old English CLAPPAN meant *to throb* or *beat*.

Clap is also a noun, a slang word for *gonnorrhoea*, a sexually transmitted disease, Swedish **gonorré**.

Klapp in Swedish has two meanings. It is *a tap*, for example, on the back or shoulder. The word is also short for **julklapp**, *Christmas present*. **Julklapp** comes from an ancient mischievous custom when people knocked on somebody's door on Christmas Eve as a joke and then threw a piece of wood or a carved doll into the hallway.

The Swedish verb **klappa** usually corresponds to English **pat**—your dog, for instance. The noun **klappa** is *a clapperboard*, two pieces of wood that are connected by a hinge and hit together before a scene when making a film, to identify each scene and to facilitate synchronizing sound and image.

class

From Latin CLASSIS, referring to *a division of the Roman people, assembly of people,* this word in both English and Swedish (**klass**) means *a category of people or things* that are differentiated from others, for example, *a social division* based on social or economic status. If you say about a person that he or she **has got class**, it means that they are *elegant* and *sophisticated*. A **class** (as well as the Swedish **klass**) is also *a group of pupils* taught together.

In English, but not in Swedish, **class** also means *lesson*, in Swedish **lektion**.

clip

A **clip** is *a flexible object* that can hold things such as banknotes, sheets of paper, etc., together, Swedish **klämma**. **Clip** also refers to *a metal holder for firearm cartridges,* Swedish **magasin**. *A short sequence* taken from a film is a **clip**, Swedish **klipp**. The verb **to clip** means *to fasten with a clip,* Swedish **fästa ihop**, or *to trim* with shears or scissors, Swedish **klippa**. The word is of West Germanic origin.

The Swedish verb **klippa** means *to cut*. The noun **klippa** means *a rock*. The noun **klipp** refers to *something cut out* from a newspaper, *a short sequence from a film*, or *a punch in a ticket*. **Att göra ett klipp** means *to make a bargain* or *bring off a big deal*.

clock

To measure time, we can use a **clock** or a **watch**. Both indicate hours, minutes, and sometimes seconds. A **clock** usually hangs on a wall or stands on the floor or on a table, etc. A **watch** is worn on the wrist or in a pocket.

The verb **clock** means *to register a specific time*. In slang, it means *to hit somebody in the face*. **Clock** comes from Medieval Latin CLOCCA, *bell*. **Watch** is from Old English WÆCCE, *watchfulness*, and WÆCCENDE, *remaining awake*, both related to WAKE.

Klocka in Swedish means both *clock, watch,* and *bell*. As in English, the word can also be used as a verb. The adjective **klockad** may refer to the bell shape of, for example, a skirt. The word is related to French CLOCHE and English CLOAK.

To ask what time it is, a Swede would say, **Hur mycket är klockan?**, which literally means **How much is the clock?** This English question of course is asked to find out the price.

The Swedish adjective **klockren** corresponds to the English expression **(as) clear as a bell** in the sense of *very clear*. It also means *perfect, precise, consummate*.

coal

Element number 6 in the Periodic System is **carbon**. Black or brown **coal** comes from carbonized plants turned into *rock*. It is used as a fuel. The word comes from Old English COL, *glowing ember*.

The Swedish word for **coal** and **carbon** is **kol**, from Old Swedish KUL.

There is another Swedish word that is pronounced in the same way but written **kål** (from Old Swedish KAL). This is Swedish for *cabbage*.

cock

Apart from meaning *a male bird* or *a tap*, this English word has a vulgar meaning, synonymous of *penis*. It comes from Old English COCC, *male bird*. The corresponding Swedish vulgar word is **kuk**, possibly from Old Norse KOKKR or KUKKER, meaning *lump* or *excrescence*, something growing out from, for example, a tree trunk. Another theory is that the word is related to **cuckoo**.

The British English **cock** for *a male bird* is **rooster** in American and Australian English.

In Swedish, a **kock** (with the same pronunciation as **cock**) is *a cook* or *chef*. The word comes from Latin COQUUS, which means *cook*.

companion

This word comes from Latin **CON-** (which changed to **COM-** because of the following **p**), *with*, and **PANIS**, *bread*. Literally, a **companion** is *someone with whom you share bread*. When you **have company**, you have a guest or guests for dinner. In modern English, a **companion** is *someone you spend a lot of time with or travel with*. Corresponding Swedish words are **följeslagare, sällskap**. The word can also refer to *one of two things that complement each other*, Swedish **pendang**, and to a book that provides information about a specific subject, *a reference book*, Swedish **handbok**.

The Swedish word **kompanjon** has the same Latin origin, but it means someone with whom you run a business, *a partner*.

compositor

A **compositor**, also called a **typographer**, *formats text and graphics* (or perhaps we should say *used to format…*) to be used in a printing process. The Swedish word is **sättare** or **typograf**. A modern **compositor** is *a computer application* that combines visual elements into an image to be shown on a computer display.

In Swedish, **kompositör** means *composer*. **Composer** and **compositor** share the same Latin origin, **COMPONERE**, *to put together*. A **compositor** puts together graphical elements, and a **composer** puts together notes to create music.

concept

In English, a **concept** is *an abstract idea*, Swedish **begrepp**, or *a plan* or *intention*, Swedish **plan**. A **concept car** is *an experimental model* to test the viability of new design features, Swedish **konceptbil**.

The Swedish word **koncept** means *rough draft, outline*. In modern language, it can have the English meaning of *idea* or *plan*, such as in **ett vinnande koncept**, *a winning concept*. **Att tappa koncepterna** means *to lose one's head*.

English **concept** and Swedish **koncept** both come from Latin CONCEPTUM, *something conceived*.

concern

In English, **concern** means *anxiety, worry*, Swedish **oro**, or *matter, business*, Swedish **angelägenhet, affär**. As a verb, it means *to have reference to*, Swedish **angå**, or *to affect, worry*, Swedish **påverka, bekymra**. The word comes from a French or late Latin word meaning *to have respect for* or *to be relevant to*.

The Swedish word **koncern** means a group of companies controlled by the same company, *a corporate group*. It has the same origin as the English word but came into Swedish from German.

concurrent

This English word means that someone or something *works in parallel or in harmony* with someone or something else, Swedish **samtidig, samverkande**. It comes from the Latin word CONCURRENTEM, *running together*. The Latin word also meant *clash, fight*.

This last meaning is found in Swedish **konkurrent**, which means *competitor*, the opposite of someone working in harmony. In the early 1500s the English verb CONCUR meant *to collide* or *clash*.

conductor

A **conductor** is a person who leads an orchestra or a choir, *a music director* or *a maestro*, Swedish **dirigent**. Another sense of **conductor** is *ticket collector*, which is also the meaning of the Swedish **konduktör**. Both words come from Latin CONDUCERE, *to bring together*, via French CONDUCTEUR.

The Swedish word **konduktor** refers to *a material that allows electricity, heat, etc., to flow through it*. This is **a conductor** in English.

confection

Confection refers to *sweets* or *candy*, Swedish **konfekt**, but can also mean *the action of mixing something*, Swedish **tillagning, tillblandning**. As a verb it means *to manufacture*, Swedish **tillverka**. The word comes from Latin CONFICERE, *put together*.

Konfektion in Swedish means *ready-made clothing*, which arguably has been put together.

consequent

If something is **consequent**, it *follows as a result of something else*, Swedish **resulterande, följande**. It comes from Middle French CONSEQUENT, originally from a Latin word meaning *to follow*.

Swedish **konsekvent** has the same origin but refers to something being *consistent* or *logical*.

conserve

Conserve means *to protect something (especially of cultural or environmental importance) from harm or destruction*, Swedish **bevara**. As a noun, **conserve** refers to *jam* or *marmalade*, Swedish **sylt, marmelad**.

The Swedish verb **konservera** usually means *to preserve, to treat food* to prevent it from decay. The plural noun **konserver** means *tinned food*. **Konservera** can also mean *to restore* (for example, paintings).

The origin of **conserve** and **konservera** is Latin CON-, *together*, and SERVARE, *to keep*.

control

In English, the verb **control** means *to rule over, to influence or determine people's behaviour*, Swedish **styra, behärska**, and the noun refers to the power of such influence. In analyses, you **control** for a variable when you make sure it is kept constant throughout a study. **Control** comes from medieval Latin CONTRAROTULUS, from CONTRA, *against*, and ROTULUS, *a small wheel*, a counter roll or register used to verify accounts, a precursor to double-entry bookkeeping, via Anglo-Norman French CONTREROLLER, *to keep a copy of a roll of accounts*.

Kontroll in Swedish (with the same Latin origin) means *check, verification*, or *domination*, and **kontrollera** is usually *to check* or *monitor* something.

cost

The noun **cost** is *the price or fee* that you pay for something, Swedish **kostnad, pris**, and the verb **cost** means *to require a payment*, a sum of money, Swedish **kosta**.

In Swedish, **kost** means *diet, food*. **Kost och logi** corresponds to *board and lodging*.

Cost and **kost** come from Latin CONSTARE, *to stand firm, stand at a price*.

costume

A **costume**, from Latin CONSUETUDO, *accustomed* (which is related to **custom**), is *a set of clothes* typical of a particular region or country or historical period, Swedish **dräkt, folkdräkt**. *A swimsuit* is also called a **bathing costume** or a **swimming costume**, Swedish **baddräkt**. **Costume** is also *what an actor wears* in a play or a film, in Swedish **kostym**.

A **fancy-dress costume**, Swedish **maskeraddräkt**, is worn at **a fancy-dress ball**, Swedish **maskeradbal**.

In Swedish, **kostym** usually refers to *a suit*, typically jacket and trousers in the same material.

court

A **court** or **court of law** acts as *a tribunal* in civil and criminal cases, Swedish **domstol**. A **court** is also *the residence and household of a king or queen*, Swedish **hov**. *An area enclosed by walls or houses* is a **court** or **courtyard**, Swedish **gård**. When a **court** is part of a castle, the Swedish word is **borggård**.

A **court** is also *an area for ballgames* such as tennis or squash, Swedish **bana**.

The verb **court** means *to be romantically involved with someone* with the intention of marrying them or *to pay special attention to someone* to try to win their support. The corresponding Swedish word is **uppvakta**.

Court comes from Latin COHORS, *yard* or *retinue*.

The Swedish noun **kort** means *card*, from Latin CHARTA, *paper, map, chart*, and the adjective **kort** means *short* or *brief*, from Latin CURTUS, *short*.

cox

This word is an abbreviation of **coxswain**, Swedish **styrman**, which means *the person who sits at the back of a rowing boat and controls the direction it moves in*. The word comes from COCKBOAT, *a small boat*, and SWAIN, *a young man*, from Old Norse SVEINN, *a lad*.

Koks in Swedish is **coke**, *the substance that is left after coal has been heated*. It is burnt to produce heat or power. Swedish has borrowed the plural form of the English word.

craft

Craft means *skill* in two areas, *adeptness* or *ability*, Swedish **skicklighet**, when making things by hand (you can talk about **craftsmanship**) and *cunning*, Swedish **list**, when it comes to deceiving others (then you are **crafty**). Old English CRÆFT came from Old German and meant *strength, skill*. **Craft** is also used to denote *boats* or *airplanes*.

The old meaning of *strength, power* is retained in Swedish **kraft**, but the Swedish word has no connotation with **cunning**. **Kraftig** in Swedish means *powerful, stout, thick-set, intense*.

cram

The English verb **cram** means *to completely fill something*, Swedish **proppa [full]**. **Cram** can also mean *to study intensively* for an exam, Swedish **plugga**. The word is of Germanic origin, in Old English CRAMMIAN, related to Dutch KRAMMEN, *to cramp*.

The Swedish noun **kram** means *a hug*. The word has the same origin as **cram**.

Kram in Swedish is also an archaic word meaning *small and cheap wares for sale*, from Middle Low German KRAM, *tent-roof, shop*.

The adjective **kram** is used about snow that is *wet and malleable* so that it can be formed into snowballs.

crass

In English, **crass** means *insensitive, not showing consideration for other people, obtuse*, Swedish **grov**, or *stupid*, Swedish **dum**.

With the same Latin origin, CRASSUS, *solid, thick*, the Swedish word **krass** usually means *materialistic, cynical*.

creature

In English, a **creature** is *an animal*, Swedish **djur**. The word can also refer to *anything created*, Swedish **varelse**, i.e., also *a human being*, Swedish **människa**. The origin is Latin CREARE, *to create*.

Kreatur in Swedish (with the same origin) means *larger farm animal, cattle, livestock*. The word can also be used as a derogatory word about human beings. In a speech in 1975, Sweden's then prime minister Olof Palme called the communist leadership of Czechoslovakia **'diktaturens kreatur'**, *'creatures of dictatorship'*.

credit

From the Latin verb CREDERE, *to believe, trust,* the noun **credit** in 16th century English meant *belief, credibility.* It now means *the ability to obtain goods or services before paying,* based on the trust that the customer will pay later. Swedish has the same word, **kredit** (with the stress on the last syllable). **Credit** also refers to *money borrowed (or lent).* **Kredit** in Swedish has the same meaning.

In bookkeeping, **credit** is *payment to an account* (the opposite of **debit**). Just as in English, the corresponding Swedish **kredit** has the stress on the first syllable. **Credit** as a verb, *to add money to an account,* is **kreditera** in Swedish.

When you **give somebody credit** for something or **credit somebody**, you *give them approval, honour, or praise* for what they have done. The Swedish phrase is **ge någon äran**.

Credits at the beginning or end of a film or television programme is *a list of contributors,* Swedish **lista över medverkande**, to the film or programme: producer, director, actors, technical staff, etc.

For completing academic courses, students get **credits** that *count towards a degree or diploma,* Swedish **kurspoäng**. In the European Credit Transfer and Accumulating System (ECTS), 60 credits represent the workload of a year of study. Credits from one university can be counted towards a qualification studied for at another university. This helps students to move between countries and have their academic qualifications and study periods abroad recognized.

The Swedish noun **kredit** only refers to *money matters* as above.

critic/critique

A **critic**, from Greek KRITES, *a judge*, via Latin CRITICUS, is *someone who criticizes* something, Swedish **kritiker**. A **critic** is also *someone who gives an opinion about books, films, music, etc.*, usually professionally. The Swedish equivalent is **kritiker** or **recensent**.

If a situation is **critical**, Swedish **kritisk**, it is *acute, serious*, or *dangerous*.

A **critique** is *a detailed analysis and assessment*, usually of a literary, philosophical, or political theory. **To critique** a theory is *to evaluate it in an analytical way*.

Kritik in Swedish means both *critique* and *criticism*, but also *review*.

crop

In English, **crop** is what you *harvest*, Swedish **skörd**. In Old English, CROPP meant *the top of a herb* and *the craw of a bird*. When you harvest, you cut off the top of a plant.

You can also **crop** something by *pruning* or *trimming* it, Swedish **beskära**. Starting in the 1930s and 1940s and then again popular in the late 1960s and early 1970s, **crop tops** were popular, cut-off shirts that exposed the waist and navel. They seem to be popular still in the 2020s. **Crop top** is **magtröja** in Swedish.

Kropp in Swedish means *body*. It probably comes from an Old Germanic word KRUBNÁ-, meaning *round object*. The word may also be related to a Greek word meaning *bent down* and *to crawl*.

cunning

A **cunning** person is *crafty, deceitful,* or *devious,* Swedish **listig**. The noun **cunning** refers to *skill in achieving something by deceit,* Swedish **list**.

Kunnig in Swedish means *skilful, competent,* or *knowledgeable.*

Cunning and **kunnig** come from Old Norse KUNNA, *know*. The sense of *deceitfulness* dates from Late Middle English; the original sense was *erudition, skill.*

cunt

This vulgar word for *a woman's genitals* can easily be misunderstood by Swedes, especially those who are not well acquainted with so-called four-letter words in English (see the **Preface** of this book). It is also used to describe a man or woman as *unpleasant, stupid,* or *contemptible*. Especially when referring to a woman, the word is highly insulting.

The word was not taboo in the Middle Ages (Middle English CUNTE) but became so in the late eighteenth century, and it was not considered fit to be printed until a hundred years later. The origin of **cunt** is unclear. It could come from Old Norse KUNTA (with the same meaning as **cunt**). Against popular belief, **cunt** is not related to the Latin word CUNNUS, *vulva*.

The corresponding vulgar Swedish word is **fitta**, whose origin is disputed. It may have come from Old Norse FIT, *beach meadow* or *moist grassland,* or Old Norse FITA, *greasy fluid, fat,* or FITJA, *rift in a rock*. In Swedish as in English, the word can also be used in a derogatory way.

The Swedish word **kant** means *edge, border, brim, fringe, rim*, etc., probably from Latin CANTHUS, *wheel-rim*.

Komma på kant with someone means *to fall out* with someone. **Hålla sig på sin kant** is *to keep to oneself, to keep aloof*. **Han är fin i kanten** means *He is oversensitive or stuck-up*.

D

dab

To **dab** someone means *to lightly pat or stroke* somebody, Swedish **klappa**, or *to apply* something lightly, Swedish **badda**. **Dab** comes from Middle English, referring to *a light striking movement*.

Dab also means *a small amount of something*, Swedish **klick**. It is also a word from the early 21st century referring to *a dance move* in hip hop. A **dab** can refer to *a flatfish, Limanda limanda*, chiefly in the North Atlantic, and *a small portion of cannabis oil*.

Dabba sig in Swedish means *to make a blunder, put one's foot in it*.

dam

A **dam** is *a barrier* built across a river to create a reservoir, Swedish **damm**. The word comes from Middle Low German or Middle Dutch.

Dam in Swedish means *lady*. **Dam** is also *the queen* in card games, chess, and draughts (or checkers). The word comes from French DAME and Latin DOMINA, *lady*.

The Swedish word **damm** has several meanings. As seen above, it corresponds to the English **dam**. **Damm** can also mean *pond* and *dike* or *dyke*. The word comes from Old Swedish DAMBER. Another sense of Swedish **damm** is *dust*.

date

A **date** is *the number of a day* in a month, Swedish **datum**. The word can also refer to a *period of time*. When you **date** something, you *specify when it happened*, was created, etc. A **date** is also *an appointment*, often a romantic one, Swedish **träff, möte**, and the corresponding verb **date** means *to go out with someone* in whom you are romantically interested. **Date** comes from Latin EPISTOLA DATA, *letter given or delivered*.

Another **date** is a sweet, oval fruit with a hard stone, Swedish **dadel**. This date comes from Greek DAKTULOS, *finger*, because of the fingerlike shape of the leaves.

Date in the sense of *appointment* is also used in Swedish, often spelled **dejt**, and the corresponding Swedish verb is **dejta** (for the spelling, see page 5).

dedication

From the Latin verb DEDICARE, *to devote* or *consecrate*, **dedication** means *commitment, enthusiasm, perseverance*, Swedish **uthållighet, entusiasm**. The English verb **dedicate** has several meanings: *to devote time or effort* to a particular task or purpose, Swedish **ägna**; *to formally open* a building or *unveil* a monument, Swedish **inviga**; *to nominate* a book, a song, etc., in somebody's honour, Swedish **tillägna, dedicera**; *to assign* a church to a saint, Swedish **helga**. A **dedication** is also *an inscription* in a book by its author to a buyer of the book, Swedish **dedikation**.

The Swedish **dedikation** only means *inscription* in a book by its author, although there now seems to be a trend among young people to use the word also in the sense of *commitment* or *enthusiasm*.

delicate

The English word **delicate** usually means *fragile, tender, exquisite,* Swedish **ömtålig, känslig, utsökt.** In Late Middle English, DELICATE meant *delightful, charming,* from French DÉLICAT and Latin DELICATUS meaning *tender, delightful, giving pleasure.* Other meanings in Middle English included *self-indulgent, fastidious,* and *effeminate.*

Swedish **delikat**, with the same origin, means *delicious.*

den

Den in English refers to *the lair* of a wild mammal, Swedish **lya**, but is also used about *a private home or hideout,* Swedish **krypin**. The word is related to German TENNE, *threshing floor.*

Den is one of the most frequent Swedish words. It is a definite or demonstrative article usually in front of an adjective or a noun, corresponding to **the** in English. **Den** also corresponds to the English personal pronoun in the third person singular, **it**.

diagram

In English, a **diagram** is *a graphic design* meant to explain something, *a drawing* that shows concepts, ideas, structures, or relations of parts, Swedish **skiss** or **figur**. Typical examples are **a circuit diagram,** Swedish **kretsschema**, **a mind map**, Swedish **mindmap**, or **a roadmap**, Swedish **vägkarta**. **Diagram** comes from two Greek words meaning *through* and *write*.

In Swedish, **diagram** refers to *bar chart, line graph,* or *pie chart*.

diligence

Diligence, Swedish **flit**, is the opposite of **laziness**, Swedish **lättja**. If you show **diligence**, you *work hard and conscientiously*. The word comes from Latin DILIGENTIA, *care, attentiveness*, from DILIGERE *to love, take delight in*.

The Swedish word **diligens** refers to *a stagecoach*. The stagecoach was an integral part of adventures in books and films about the Wild West. It was a covered, horse-drawn carriage for passengers and mail on established routes between small towns, usually to a regular schedule. The word comes from French VOÎTURE (or CARROSSE) DE DILIGENCE, *vehicle* (or *coach*) *of speed*, in the late 1700s, when the stagecoach was a common means of travelling in France and other countries.

direct

Contrary to English **direct**, *to order, to control or be in charge of*, Swedish **styra, leda**; *to aim*, Swedish **rikta**; *to instruct actors in a film or play*,

Swedish **regissera**, the Swedish word **direkt** is not used as a verb but, as also in English, as an adjective or an adverb, *straight, immediately*. For the etymology of **direct/direkt**, see **direction**.

direction

The Latin noun DIRECTIO comes from the verb DIRIGERE, from DI-, *distinctly*, or DE-, *down*, and RIGERE, *to put straight*.

Direction refers to *the point towards which someone or something moves or is facing*, Swedish **riktning**. It also means *a line of action* or *instruction*, Swedish **anvisning**. The word can also refer to *management* or *administration*, Swedish **ledning, direktion**.

In Swedish, **direktion** only refers to *management* or *administration*.

disc, disk

A **disc** or **disk,** Swedish **skiva,** is *a flat, thin round ob*ject such as a musical record. A **disk** can be used to store information that can be read by a computer.

Disk also refers to *a small piece of cartilage* between the bones in your back.

The word comes from French DISQUE and Latin DISCUS, *disk*, originally from Greek DISKOS, derived from the verb DISKEIN, *to throw*.

In Swedish, apart from the disk in your back, **disk** has two meanings, *counter* and *washing-up*. The Swedish word has the same Latin origin.

When you wash the dishes, you clean the round plates. In Old Swedish, DISKER meant *plate, dish,* and *table*. This is related to English **desk**. Latin DISCUS also meant *table*.

discrete

The English adjective **discrete** means *separate, having a clear independent form,* Swedish **åtskild**. It comes from Latin DISCRETUS, *separate,* from the verb DISCERNERE, *to separate*.

Discrete mathematics deals with objects that are separated from each other into distinct parts.

Swedish **diskret** means *discreet, tactful, reticent*.

disposition

In English, **disposition** refers to *a person's mood, character, or inclination,* Swedish **temperament, läggning**.

Disposition also means *the way in which something is arranged,* Swedish **arrangemang**. If you **have something at your disposition**, you *can deal with it as you please*.

In Swedish, **disposition** means *disposal, outline, arrangement,* or *predisposition*.

Disposition comes from the Latin verb DISPONERE, *to arrange*.

diverse

When things are **diverse**, they are *very different*, Swedish **olika**. The word can also refer to *people from different social and ethnic backgrounds, different genders*, etc., Swedish **mångfaldig**.

In Swedish, **diverse** means *sundry, various*.

Diverse comes from Latin DIVERSE from the verb DIVERTERE, *to turn in separate ways*.

dog

A **dog**, from Old English DOCGA, of unknown origin, is a four-legged animal, *a pet*, Swedish **hund**. The verb **dog** means *to follow somebody closely*. A **dog** is also slang for *an unpleasant man* or *unattractive woman*.

Dog in Swedish is the past tense of **dö**, *to die*.

drag

The English verb **drag**, Swedish **dra**, **släpa**, from Old Norse DRAGA, *to draw*, means *to pull or draw* something or somebody forcefully or with difficulty or *to take someone somewhere against their will*. Used about time, it means *to pass slowly*. You can **drag** an image across a display screen with a mouse.

As a noun, **drag** means *a force that acts against the forward movement* of something, Swedish **motstånd**. Drag can also refer to someone (or something) that is *boring or unpleasant*, Swedish **tråkmåns**. Cars or motorcycles can compete against each other in a **drag race**. A **drag queen** is a man dressed as a woman, usually for entertainment. A **drag** is *something that is dragged along the bottom* of, for example, a lake when searching for a dead body, Swedish **dragg**. As a verb, it refers to that action.

Drag in Swedish is a noun meaning *a tug or pull, a strain, a feature or characteristic,* or *a draught*. In board games, **drag** is *a move*. In sport fishing, **drag** is *a trolling-spoon*. **Drag race** and **drag queen** have also come into the Swedish language.

duke

A **duke**, Swedish **hertig**, is a man holding *the highest hereditary title in the British nobility*. The word comes from Latin DUX, *leader*.

Duk in Swedish means *tablecloth* or a painter's *canvas*. The word comes from Old Saxon and Middle Low German DÔK.

dumb

A **dumb** person is *unable to speak*, Swedish **stum**. Especially in colloquial North American English, **dumb** also means *stupid*. The word is of Germanic origin, related to Old Norse DUMBR.

Dum in Swedish means *stupid, foolish, annoying*. **Inte så dum** means *not bad*. The Swedish word **damm** has the same pronunciation as **dumb**; it means *dam, dyke, pond,* or *dust*.

dunk

To **dunk** is *to dip*, for example, a biscuit or a piece of bread, into a soup or a drink or *to immerse something* in a liquid, Swedish **doppa**. The word came into English in the early 1900s from Pennsylvanian German TUNKEN, *to dip*. In basketball, **dunk** means *to score a goal* with your hands above the rim, Swedish **dunka**.

Dunk in Swedish is *a can* or *drum* for liquids. The word also refers to *a thump, throb,* or *clunk*. **Dunk** comes from Dutch TONNEKE or North German TUNNEKE, *small barrel*.

dust

Dust is *a fine powder of dry dirt*, Swedish **damm** or **stoft**. The verb **dust**, Swedish **damma**, refers to what you do when you *remove dust*. The verb can also mean the opposite, *to sprinkle a powdered substance* on to something, Swedish **strö, pudra**.

Dust is of Germanic origin and came into Old English. It is related to Dutch DUIST, *chaff*.

The Swedish word **dust** means *fight, tussle,* or *clash*. In the Middle Ages, **dust** referred to a fight between two knights on horseback. The word comes from Old French JOSTER, *to get together, clash*, originally from Latin JUXTA, *beside, next to*.

E

effective

When something is **effective,** Swedish **verksam, effektfull**, it *gives the result that was intended*. It tells us whether something has been done, not how it was done. The focus is on the result. **Effective** can also indicate that something is *valid* or *in force*, for example, from a certain date, Swedish **giltig, gällande**. The word comes from the Latin verb EFFICERE, *accomplish*.

The Swedish word **effektiv** means *efficient*. When something is efficient, it works well without wasting time, money, or energy. **Effektiv** can also mean *actual, real*.

engaged

To be **engaged** means *to be busy* or *occupied,* Swedish **upptagen**. You can also be **engaged to be married,** Swedish **förlovad**. To **engage** somebody is *to hire or take somebody into employment,* Swedish **anställa**. The clutch of a car can **engage,** *move into position to operate,* Swedish **kopplas in**. The word comes from French ENGAGER, *to pledge something, to pledge oneself to do something, to enter into a contract*.

If you are **engagerad** in Swedish, you are *committed* or *dedicated*. As in English, the word can also mean *busy* or *hired*.

entrée

From the French ENTRÉE meaning *entry* or *access*, originally referring to the opening act of an opera or a musical, **entrée** in British English means *starter course* or the *dish before the main course* on a menu; in North American English it refers to *the main course* or *the only course*. **Entrée** can also refer to the right to join a particular group.

In Swedish, **entré** means *entrance [to a building], entry [on a stage], admission,* or *entrance fee*.

entrepreneur

English **entrepreneur** and Swedish **entreprenör** share the same meaning of *businessperson, manager, founder,* but the Swedish word often also means *contractor*. English and Swedish have the same origin, a 13th century French verb ENTREPRENDRE, *to do something, undertake*.

esplanade

From Latin EXPLANATUS, *flattened, levelled,* **esplanade** in English meant *an open space between a fortress and a town*. Nowadays, an **esplanade** is *a wide path for walking,* usually along the sea. The corresponding Swedish word is **strandpromenad**.

In Swedish, **esplanad** refers to *an avenue* or *boulevard, a wide street,* usually with trees in the middle.

etiquette

The French word ÉTIQUETTE referred to a list of rules on *how to behave* at a court. Both the English **etiquette** and the Swedish **etikett** mean *the code or unwritten law of polite behaviour* between people in the same group.

In Swedish, **etikett** also means *label*. French ÉTIQUETTE comes from ESTIQUETTE meaning *short written note* and *licence or permit*. This is where English **ticket** comes from.

even

In English, **even** has several meanings: *totally flat, not changing, divided equally,* or *equally balanced,* Swedish **jämn**. The word is also used as a verb, *to make even,* Swedish **jämna [ut]**. **Even** can also be used *to emphasize something,* as in **This was even better** or **We all liked it, even Dad**. This **even** is **till och med** in Swedish.

Even is used about *numbers that are divisible by two* without a remainder, Swedish **jämn**.

Even as means *at the very same time as.*

Även in Swedish means *also, too, likewise, as well.* **Även om** means *even if.*

Even and **även** have the same Proto-Germanic origin *EBNAZ.

eventually

We will eventually do it means that *we will do it finally, sooner or later*, Swedish **till slut**.

In Swedish, **vi ska eventuellt göra det** means that *we will possibly do it*. As you can see, this word can easily be misunderstood. The English word tells us that something will definitely happen, even if it may take some time, while the Swedish word indicates that it is uncertain whether it will happen at all. However, English **eventuality** means a *possible event or outcome*.

The Latin verb EVENIRE meant *to come out, happen, result*.

execution

Execution in English means *implementation or carrying out* of a plan, etc. The word can also refer to *the rendition* or *delivery* of a piece of art such as a painting or a piece of music. Both meanings are **utförande** in Swedish. As a law term, **execution** means *the putting into effect* of a will or other legal instrument, Swedish **verkställande**.

Execution is also *the carrying out of a death sentence* or *the killing of someone* as a political act.

Exekution in Swedish only refers to *capital punishment* or *the killing of someone* as above.

The English and Swedish words have the same Latin origin, EX-, *out*, and SEQUI, *to follow*.

exercise

Exercise is *an activity* carried out for a specific purpose, usually to improve health. As a verb, **exercise** means *to engage in physical activity* or *to apply,* for example, *authority*. An **exercise** is also *an assignment or a task* in order to practise a skill. *A military drill or training* is an **exercise**. The corresponding Swedish word is **övning**. **Exercise** comes from Latin EXCERCERE, *to keep busy, practise, train.*

Exercis in Swedish means *military drill and discipline.* In colloquial language, now old-fashioned, it used to refer to *compulsory military service.*

expedition

An **expedition** is *a journey for a specific purpose,* such as exploring a country, etc., or *a military campaign.* **Expedition** can also mean *speed* in doing something. To **expedite** is *to quicken something, to accelerate the progress of something.*

In Swedish, in addition to a journey undertaken by explorers, **expedition** means *office.* **Godsexpedition** is *a goods or freight office.*

The word comes from Latin EXPEDITIO, *an enterprise against an enemy.*

F

fabric

Fabric usually refers to *textile material* that has been woven or knitted, Swedish **tyg**. It can also refer to *the structure of a building*, Swedish **stomme**, and figuratively to *the basic structure of a culture, society, etc.*, Swedish **uppbyggnad, struktur**. The word comes from Latin FABRICA, *something skillfully produced.*

In Swedish, **fabrik** means *factory* or *plant*—where things are produced, usually skillfully.

familiar

Familiar, from Latin FAMILIA, *household servants, family*, means *well known, customary*, Swedish **bekant**. It can also mean *intimate*.

Swedish **familjär** only means *intimate* or *overly friendly*.

famous

Someone who is **famous** is *well-known* or *renowned*, Swedish **berömd**. The word comes from Latin FAMOSUS, *much talked of.* In colloquial language, the English word can also mean *excellent, first-rate*.

Famös in Swedish has a more negative meaning of *infamous, notorious*. It has the same Latin origin but came into Swedish from French FAMEUX.

fan

Both English and Swedish use this word, coming from FANATIC, in the sense of *admirer, aficionado,* or *enthusiast*. In English, the word also refers to something used to cool, for example, a room or a person, Swedish **fläkt**. This **fan** comes from Latin VANNUS, a *winnowing fan*.

The Swedish word **fan** is an expletive or curse referring to *the devil*. It most likely comes from Old Norse FJENDEN, FAENDIN, or FENDINN, *enemy*. In English, **fiend** means *devil*, but also—surprise, surprise!—*fanatic*.

See also **fiend**.

far

This English word comes from Old English FEOR or FEORR, *at a great distance* or *long ago*. The modern word is related to distance, Swedish **långt**.

In Swedish, **far** means *father*. It is short for **fader**, which is a formal and archaic form from Proto-Indo-European *PHTÉR, *father*, via Proto-Germanic *FADER, related to Latin PATER and Sanskrit PITAR.

fart

Fart is what you do when you let out gas through your anus or the sound of that action. A nicer way to express this is to say *to break wind*, which is what the original Old English FEORTAN meant. The Swedish word for the noun is **prutt**, **fjärt**, or **fis**.

If you call someone **an old fart** in English, you think the person is *boring* or *annoying*.

As we have seen in the **Introduction**, the Swedish (and Scandinavian) word **fart** means *velocity*, *speed*, or *travel*. It comes from the Low German verb FAREN, *travel*.

Farthinder is the Swedish word for *speed bump*. **Infart** is *entrance*, **utfart** is *exit from a building*, **avfart** is *exit from a motorway*, **påfart** is *entrance to a motorway, acceleration lane*, and **uppfart** is *driveway* (for vehicles). **Luftfart** is *aviation*. **Farthållare** means *cruise control*, **fartkamera** is *speed camera*, and **maxfart** is *top speed*. If you are **fartblind**, *speed blind*, you don't realize that you are driving too fast—you have got used to the high speed.

Elevators in Denmark often have a sign saying **I fart** meaning *under way*. An anecdote says that, during a visit by Queen Elizabeth II, somebody realized just in time what the sign meant in English, and it was rapidly covered up.

fast

The English adjective **fast** means *moving (or capable of moving) at a high speed*, Swedish **snabb**. The word is also used to say that a watch or clock is showing a time ahead of the correct time. **Fast** can also mean *steadily fastened, firm, fixed*.

The adverb **fast** has two meanings, *rapidly* and *firmly*.

English **fast** has a Germanic origin; in Old English it was FÆSTE, *firmly*.

As a verb, **fast** means *to go without food*. The verb originally meant *to stick to [certain religious precepts]*. The corresponding Swedish verb is **fasta**. English **Lent** is **fastan** in Swedish.

Fast in Swedish has the English meaning of *solid, firm,* or *fixed*, but it can also mean *stuck*. The word is also a subjunction (a word that links clauses or sentences) meaning *though, although*.

Faster in Swedish is *an aunt*, your father's sister. Your mothers' sister is your **moster**.

fat

The noun **fat** in English refers to an *oily animal or vegetable substance* or *grease*. As an adjective used about people, it means *plump, overweight,* or *obese*. It can also be used about things that are *large in circumference*. **Fat** is of West Germanic origin.

Fat in Swedish means a *vat* or *barrel*. It is also a *measure of liquids*, about 157 litres. (A barrel of petroleum measures 200 litres. An English barrel has 159 litres.)

Another sense of **fat** in Swedish is *plate* or *dish*. **Tefat** (literally *tea plate*) is the Swedish word for *saucer*, and **askfat** is *an ashtray*. **Tvättfat** or **handfat** is *a wash basin*. **Fatöl** is *draught beer*.

fawn

A **fawn** is *a young deer*, Swedish **hjortkalv, kid**. The word also refers to *a light brown colour*, Swedish **ljust gulbrun**. As a verb, **fawn** means *to give birth to a deer*, Swedish **kalva**. The word comes from Latin FETUS, *offspring*, via Old French FAON.

Another meaning of the verb **fawn** is *to flatter someone* in order to gain favour, Swedish **fjäska**. This **fawn** comes from Old English FAGNIAN, *to make glad* or *be glad*.

With the same pronunciation as **fawn**, Swedish **fån** means *a fool*. The word comes from Norwegian FÅ, *quiet, reticent*. It is often used in the phrase **Jag stod där som ett fån**, *I stood there like a fool*.

feel

When you **feel**, *you experience something* physical or emotional or *touch something* in order to discover something about it, Swedish **känna**. **Feel** also means *to have an opinion or consider* something. As a noun, **feel** refers to *the way something feels* or *a touch to examine something*, Swedish **känsla**. When you **have a feel** for something, you *have a natural understanding* of it.

If you **feel like** doing something, you *have a desire* to do it, Swedish **ha lust**.

Feel is of West Germanic origin, in Old English FELAN.

With roughly the same pronunciation, Swedish **fil** has several meanings. **Fil** or **filmjölk** is a fermented milk product, *sour milk*. **Fil** is also *a row or line* of people or things or *a lane* on a road. The word comes from Latin FILUM, thread. **Fil** also corresponds to *a computer file* in English. Another **fil** is *a tool* to smoothen or shape, for example, metal or wood.

fell

The English verb **fell** means *to cut down*, e.g., a tree, Swedish **fälla**. Figuratively, the word means *to knock down* or *topple* someone. It is of Germanic origin.

Fell, Swedish **föll**, is also the past simple of the verb **fall**.

Fäll in Swedish is *an animal's hide or skin with its hair*. The word comes from an Indo-European root and was PELLIS, *skin*, in Latin. It is related to an archaic English word **fell**.

fester

The English verb **fester** is used about *a wound becoming septic*, Swedish **vara sig**, or *about food becoming rotten*, Swedish **ruttna**. Figuratively, it refers to *negative feelings becoming worse*, Swedish **orsaka bitterhet, ligga**

och gnaga. **Fester** comes from Latin FISTULA, *pipe, reed, fistula*, which later became *festering sore* in Late Middle English.

Fester in Swedish is the plural form of **fest**, *party*. The word comes from Latin FESTUM, *festival, banquet, feast*.

fiend

A **fiend** is *a devil, an evil spirit*, or *a very wicked or cruel person*, Swedish **djävul, ond ande**. The word also refers to *an enthusiast or supporter* of, for example, a football team, Swedish **fan, fanatiker**. FEOND, from a Germanic verb meaning *hate*, meant *enemy, devil, demon* in Old English.

With the same origin, **fiende** in Swedish has retained the old sense of *enemy*.

See also **fan**.

figure

A **figure** is a number and a numerical symbol, such as 1, 2, 3, etc., Swedish **siffra, tal**. The word also refers to *a geometric shape* or *an illustrative drawing*, Swedish **figur**. A **figure** can be *a person seen as an outline or silhouette*, and the word is used especially about *the bodily shape of a woman*. In Latin, FIGURA meant *shape, form*.

Figur in Swedish has the same meanings as in English except for the reference to *number*.

filial

Filial, from Latin FILIUS, *son*, and FILIA, *daughter*, means *relating to a son or daughter*, Swedish **sonlig, dotterlig**. You can talk about **filial respect** or **filial affection**.

The Swedish noun **filial** is business language and refers to *a branch*, i.e., a part of a large business organization.

first floor

In British English, **first floor** refers to *the floor that is one level above the ground floor* of a building.

In Swedish as in American English, **första våningen** and **first floor**, respectively, refer to *the ground floor*. **Bottenvåningen**, literally **the bottom floor**, is another Swedish word for *the ground floor*.

fit

Fit meaning *proper or suitable*, Swedish **lämplig, passande**, is from Late Middle English of unknown origin. In the sense of *in condition, physically fit*, Swedish **spänstig, i form**, the word is from the second half of the 19th century.

Fit for fight is a pseudo-English expression sometimes used by Swedes. The correct English version is **fighting fit,** Swedish **i toppform**.

The noun **fit** refers to *a sudden attack of convulsions* or *sudden uncontrollable laughter, etc.*, Swedish **anfall**. This **fit** comes from Old English FIT, *conflict*; the sense of *sudden attack of illness* is from the mid-16th century.

As a verb, **fit** means *to be of the right size and shape* or *to join to form a whole*, Swedish **passa [in]**.

Fitta, as we have seen above, is a Swedish vulgar word for **cunt**.

flak

Flak comes from German FLIEGERABWEHRKANONE, *aviator-defence gun*, and refers to *anti-aircraft fire*, Swedish **luftvärn**. **Flak** is also *strong criticism* or *blame*, Swedish **kritik, ogillande**.

Flak in Swedish has two meanings, *[lorry] platform, flatbed*, and *[ice] floe*. **Ett flak öl** is a *flat of beer*, a case of 24 cans or bottles of beer. Swedish **flak** is possibly from Proto-Indo-European *PEL-, *broad, wide, flat*.

flat

The adjective **flat** means *having a level surface, shallow, monotonous, not varied, sluggish, punctured*, and *lacking contrast*. This **flat** comes from Old Norse FLATR.

In a music score, **flat** is *a note lowered a semitone*, Swedish **sänkt med en halvton**.

♭
A flat symbol

A **flat of beer**, as we saw above, is *a case of 24 beers*, Swedish **flak**.

A **flat**, Swedish **lägenhet**, in British and Australian English corresponds to an **apartment** in American English, i.e., *a set of rooms*, usually on the same floor and in a larger building, a block of flats. Of Germanic origin, in the early 19th century **flat** denoted *a floor* or *storey*.

Swedish **flat** shares the meaning of *having a level surface* with English **flat**, but it also means *weak, indulgent,* and *taken aback, flabbergasted*.

Flata in Swedish means *the flat side* of something. **Handflata** is *the palm of your hand*.

In colloquial Swedish, **flata** is *a female homosexual, a lesbian, a dyke*, possibly referring to the shape of the genitals of the female body. It was originally an offensive word but has now been reclaimed by the gay rights movement.

fond

Fond means *affectionate, loving,* Swedish **tillgiven, förtjust**. It can also mean *infatuated, naive, unrealistic,* Swedish **fåfäng**, as in **a fond hope**. The word comes from Middle English FON, *fool, be foolish*.

In Swedish, **fond** is a noun with several meanings. It can mean *fund* or *foundation*. It can mean *funds, capital,* or *fortune*. In a theatre, **fond** is the *backdrop* or *background*. In cooking, **fond** means *stock*. The Latin origin FUNDUS meant *bottom*.

fort

Fort is a partial false friend in English and Swedish. The two languages share the meaning of *fortified place, stronghold* from Latin FORTIS, *strong*, but in Swedish, the word is also an adverb meaning *fast, rapidly*.

foster

Foster, Swedish **fostra**, means *to encourage the development of something, to develop a feeling or idea in oneself*, or *to bring up a child*. In Old English, FOSTRIAN meant *to feed, nourish*, of Germanic origin.

The Swedish noun **foster** means *foetus* or, figuratively, *creation, product*, from Old English FOSTOR, *bringing up, breeding*.

friend

The English word **friend,** Swedish **vän**, refers to *somebody whom you know well and like very much* but is not a relative.

Frände is an archaic word in Swedish meaning *relative* or *fellow countryman*.

Friend and **frände** both come from a Proto-Germanic word meaning *to love*. Indo-European languages often had the same word for *friend* and *relative*. English retained the sense of friend and Swedish that of relative.

frisk

To **frisk** in English is *to search* for drugs, hidden weapons, etc., on somebody by passing the hands over the person, Swedish **muddra**. Frisk was a slang word in the late 18th century. In the sense *to leap joyfully* (about a dog, for example), the word comes from Old French FRISQUE, *alert, lively, merry*. The corresponding Swedish verb is **skutta** or **hoppa**.

Frisk in Swedish is an adjective meaning *healthy, sound, well*, as well as *fresh*, from Middle Low German VRISCH.

from

From in English is a preposition to indicate the point in time or space at which something starts, Swedish **från**. From was in Old Norse FRÁ and in Old English FRAM.

The Swedish word **from** is an adjective meaning *pious, devout,* or *gentle*. It comes from Old Saxon FRUMA.

fuck

Fuck, meaning *sexual intercourse* or *to have sexual intercourse,* is one of so-called four-letter words in English, colloquial or vulgar words for genitals and sexual activity. There are various theories about the origin of **fuck**. It could come from Norwegian dialectal FUKKA, *to copulate,* or from Middle English FYKE or FIKE, *to move restlessly* or *flirt*. The German equivalent to **fuck**, FICKEN, originally meant *to flick, move back and forth*. The corresponding Swedish vulgar word is **knulla**.

There is a Swedish word **fack**, with the same pronunciation as **fuck**. The Swedish word means *compartment, box,* or *safe*. Another meaning is *branch, trade*.

Fack is also an abbreviation of **fackförening,** *trade union.* **Facklitteratur** is *specialist literature, non-fiction,* **fackspråk** is *technical jargon,* and a **fackman** is *an expert* who is **fackkunnig,** *skilled* or *experienced*.

A hotel receptionist should not be surprised if a Swedish tourist innocently asks, **'Can I have a fack for my money?'** And a trade union official might invite a new employee to **'join the fack'**.

full

Full in English has many synonyms: *complete, crowded, abounding,* etc. It is from an old Germanic word. The most common antonym is **empty**.

Full in Swedish shares many meanings with the English word, but when English uses **full** to mean that *you have eaten a lot* and cannot eat more, which is **mätt** in Swedish, the Swedish adjective **full** (as well as colloquial Australian English **full**) means that *you are drunk* or *intoxicated*.

fur

Fur is *the short hair* of some animals, Swedish **päls**. **Fur** comes from Old French FORRE, *sheath*. In modern English slang, a **furu** is a *fake guru* or *con man*, giving advice on the internet with the aim of inducing people to invest money in doubtful enterprises.

Fur or **fura** in Swedish is a tree, *a [long-boled] pine*, Latin *Pinus*. Another Swedish word for *pine* is **tall**. **Furu** refers to *pinewood*. This **fur** is of Germanic origin.

See also **tall**.

fusion

A **fusion** is *melting together*, Swedish **sammansmältning**. This can refer to *the joining* of metals to form a new metal or *the combination of nuclei of atoms*. In music it means *a mixture* of different styles, such as jazz and rock. The same can apply to cooking styles. The word comes from Latin FUNDERE, *to pour* or *melt*.

In addition to nuclear fusion and music style, the Swedish word **fusion** is used in business language meaning *merger*, the combination of companies into one company.

G

gage

In English, **gage** refers to *a pledge*, something deposited as security that an obligation will be fulfilled, Swedish **pant**. The verb **gage** means *to offer something as a guarantee of good faith*, Swedish **sätta i pant**. **Gage** can also mean *a glove* thrown on the ground as a challenge to fight, Swedish **stridshandske**. The word comes from Old French GAGE and GAGER, of Germanic origin.

Gage is the American English spelling of **gauge**, *measure*, Swedish **mäta** (verb) and **mått** (noun).

Gage in Swedish means *fee*, a sum of money paid to an artist to perform. The word comes from French GAGE, *pledge, pay*, originally from Medieval Latin VADIUM, *pledge*.

gang

English **gang**, Swedish **gäng**, usually refers to *an organized group of criminals*; its members are called **gangsters**. Such a criminal organization is also called a **mafia, mob, outfit,** or **syndicate**. **Gang** can also refer to *team, band, company, clique*, etc. The word is of Germanic origin meaning *going, journey*. In Old English it meant *journey, way, passage*, in Middle English *way* or *set of things or people that go together*.

The Swedish word **gång** has the same Germanic origin. It has several meanings. Going back to its origin, it means *walking* or *gait*. It can also mean *passage, corridor,* and *aisle*. The word is also used to mean *time* as in *the first (last, second, third, etc.) time*.

gem

A **gem** in English is *a jewel*, a *precious stone,* Swedish **ädelsten, juvel**. The word comes from Latin GEMMA, *bud, jewel*.

A Swedish **gem** is *a paper clip,* obviously of much lower value than an English **gem**. The word comes from a machine that would make wire paper clips. The machine was invented in 1899 by William Middlebrook for the Gem Company in England.

genera

Genera is the plural of **genus**, a taxonomic category between *species* and *family,* Swedish **släkte**. **Genus** came into English in the mid 16th century from Latin GENUS, *birth, race, stock*.

Genera in Swedish is a verb meaning *to bother, embarrass, trouble*. If you are **generad** in Swedish, you are *embarrassed, self-conscious*. This word comes from French GÊNER, *to torment, torture, harass,* originally from the French noun GÊNE, *a torture to extort a confession*.

general

As an adjective, this English word means *not exact, not detailed, widespread, common, normal*. This is in Swedish **allmän, generell**. The word is used in titles such as **Secretary General**, Swedish **generalsekreterare**, **Director General, General Manager**, both **generaldirektör** in Swedish, etc. The noun **general** is also *a high military rank*. It comes from Latin GENERALIS, from GENUS, *class, race, kind*, via French CAPITAINE GÉNÉRAL, *commander-in-chief*.

Apart from titles such as those mentioned above, **general** in Swedish only refers to the military rank; the Swedish adjective is **generell**.

genial

The English adjective **genial** means *friendly, amiable*, Swedish **vänlig, sympatisk, gemytlig**. It comes from Latin GENIALIS, *productive*. In the 17th century the word meant *mild and conducive to growth* in English.

A rare meaning of **genial** is *relating to the chin*, from Greek GENUS, *jaw*.

The Swedish adjective **genial** means *brilliant, ingenious*.

get

This English verb has several synonyms, such as *to receive, attain, achieve, obtain, experience, become, come, persuade, understand*, etc. Swedish equivalents are **få, bli, fatta**. In Old Norse, GETA meant *to obtain, beget,* *guess*. **Get** is related to Old English GIETAN, which is found in FORGIETAN, *to forget*. The word comes from an Indo-European root.

In Swedish, **get** is a noun meaning *goat*, Latin *Capra hircus*.

gift

The English noun **gift** means *present*, something you give, Swedish **gåva, present**. In Old English (from Old Norse), GIFT meant *giving, consideration, dowry,* and *wedding*. The Indo-European origin was GHEBH-

As a verb, especially in journalism, **to gift** something to somebody implies that the receiver does not have to make an effort to get it.

If you are **gifted**, Swedish **begåvad**, you are *talented*.

In Swedish, **gift** has two very different meanings, *poison* (or *venom*) and *married*. This would make a perfect joke for a stand-up comedian. In fact, the Swedish word has the same origin as the English word. A father could **gifta** his daughter in marriage. **Hemgift** is the Swedish word for *dowry* (which, by the way, comes from a Latin word related to **give**).

Swedish **gift** in the sense of *poison* or *venom* probably comes from *a giving, a portion prescribed,* sometimes used to mean an *amount of medicine*. From there, the Scandinavian, German, and Dutch **gift** meaning *poison* may have emerged.

gill

A **gill** is *the breathing organ of a fish* (Swedish **gäl**). The word comes from Old Norse. If you are **green around the gills**, you feel *nauseous*.

A **gill** is also *a quarter of a pint,* from Latin GILLO, *water pot.*

In Northern English, a **gill** (or **ghyll**), from Old Norse GILL, *deep glen,* is *a deep ravine* or *a narrow mountain stream.*

Finally, **gill** or **jill** is *a female ferret*. The word is also used in a derogatory way about *a young woman*. It comes from a Middle English given name, GILLIAN.

In Swedish, **gill** is a law term meaning *valid* from Old Icelandic and Old Norwegian GILDR, from a Proto-Germanic word meaning *that which should be paid.*

Gilla is a Swedish verb meaning *to like, appreciate,* and *accept.*

glass

Glass, Swedish **glas**, is *the transparent substance* that windows and drinking containers are made of. The word, of Germanic origin, was GLÆS in Old English.

The Swedish noun **glass** means *ice-cream*. It comes from French GLACE, *ice.*

god

In monotheistic religions such as Christianity, **God**, Swedish **Gud,** is a *deity,* the supreme being, the creator of the universe. The word is also used as an exclamation to express surprise, anger, etc.

In Swedish, **god** is an adjective meaning *good, excellent, satisfactory,* as well as *kind, nice.*

Gods in Swedish means *goods, material, freight,* or *property*. The word also refers to *a manor* or *estate.* **Godsexpedition** means *goods office* or *freight forwarding.*

gracious

The English word **gracious** means *merciful, kind, friendly,* Swedish **nådig, älskvärd**, and *elegant, stylish,* Swedish **elegant**. It comes from a Latin word meaning *esteem, favour.*

The word is sometimes used as an exclamation of surprise: **Good gracious**, I didn't expect you here!

The Swedish **graciös** only means *graceful, elegant.*

grave

The English adjective **grave** comes from Latin GRAVIS, *heavy, serious*. It means *serious, solemn,* Swedish **allvarlig, högtidlig**.

The noun **grave**, meaning *a hole in the ground for a coffin or a dead body* comes from Old English GRAEF, which is related to German **GRAB**, *grave*. The corresponding Swedish noun is **grav**. To **bury** is **begrava** in Swedish.

The adjective **grav** is relatively seldom used in Swedish, except in expressions such as **en grav anklagelse**, *a serious accusation*.

The verb **gräva** means *to dig*. **Vallgrav** is the Swedish word for *moat*.

The Swedish adjective **gravid**, *pregnant, expecting a baby*, also comes from Latin GRAVIS, *heavy*.

groove

The noun **groove** refers to *a long, narrow cut* in a hard material such as the track on a gramophone record, Swedish **spår**. Metaphorically, **groove** means *an established routine*. Particularly in jazz slang, if you are **in the groove**, you are *performing very well* or *enjoying yourself*, Swedish **i toppform**, while dancing or listening to music.

Groove comes from Dutch GROEVE, *furrow, pit*.

The Swedish adjective **grov** means *coarse, rough* or *big, heavy*. It comes from Indo-European GHRUBH. **Ett grovt brott** is *a serious crime*.

guilty

If you are **guilty**, you have *broken the law* and should be punished. **Guilty** can also mean that *you feel ashamed* and have a bad conscience because of some wrongdoing. Old English GYLT meant *crime, sin, failure of duty*. **Guilty** is **skyldig** in Swedish.

The Swedish word **giltig** means *valid,* from German GELTEN, *to be valid.*

gymnasium

An English **gymnasium** is *a place where you do gymnastics* or other physical exercises. The Swedish equivalent is **gymnastiksal** or **gym**.

In Sweden, a **gymnasium** is a school that prepares pupils for university entrance, corresponding to *upper secondary* or *senior high school.*

In Latin a GYMNASIUM meant both *a place of education* and *a place for exercise*. The Greek word GUMNOS meant *naked* and GUMNASION *exercise*. A gymnasium was a school for naked exercise. English has retained the meaning of *exercise* and Swedish that of *school*.

H

halt

From German HALTEN, *to hold*, **halt** in English means *to bring or come to a sudden stop*. The word is also used as *a military command* to bring marching troops to a stop. **Halt** also means *a pause, intermission,* or *break*. In archaic English it also meant *limp* and *limping*.

Halt in Swedish has the same origin and meaning of *Stop!*, but it has three additional meanings. **Halt** refers to *the percentage of content* in something, such as sugar in juice, etc., as well as *substance, worth, intrinsic value*. **Halt** also means *limping, lame*. As an adjective modifying a neuter noun, **halt** means *slippery*.

hammock

In English, **hammock** is *a thin bed*, usually of canvas, that is hung between two supports, in Swedish **hängmatta**, literally *hanging mat*. The hammock was first invented by people in the Caribbean for sleeping. The word comes via Spanish HAMACA from an Arawakan (Haitian) word meaning *fish nets*. Christopher Columbus brought it to Europe.

Just as **hammock** in English is a loanword from Spanish, Swedish **hammock** is a loanword from English, but it refers to the English *garden swing* or *porch swing*. The word has been adapted to Swedish grammar; the plural is **hammockar**.

hamstring

A **hamstring** is *a tendon* at the back of a knee, Swedish **knäsena**. As a verb, it is used figuratively, *to disable, to limit or severely restrict the ability to do something*, Swedish **lamslå**. In Old English, **ham** or **hom** denoted *the back of the knee*, from a Germanic word that meant *to be crooked*.

Hamstring in Swedish has a completely different meaning. It refers to *hoarding*, accumulating and storing money or necessaries, especially in times of war or economic depression. The word comes from the habit of hamsters of gathering large reserves of food. It was introduced in Swedish newspapers during World War I. The corresponding verb is **hamstra**.

handicapped

The word **handicap** is from the 17th century. Its etymology has been explained by Ron Amundson at the University of Hawaii at Hilo. **Handicap** comes from a game between two traders. Each of the two traders offered an item for sale and put some forfeit money in a hat or cap. An umpire decided on the difference in value between the two items, which was called *the boot* or *odds*. The traders put their hands in the hat or cap and then removed them to indicate their willingness to trade by showing an open or a closed hand.

Around 1750 the word **handicap** began to be used in horse races. Two horses carried different weights to equalize their chances of winning. Matchmakers became known as **handicappers** and the race **a handicap**. The word **handicap** still did not apply to disadvantages but to the contest. However, it later came to be used metaphorically about disadvantages. In 1915 the word was first used to designate *mental or physical impairment.*

Swedish **handikappad** and English **handicapped** are no longer preferred. Instead, other words are used in English such as *disabled, impaired, physically challenged, paraplegic,* etc. In Swedish, **handikappad** has been replaced by words meaning *functionally impaired, intellectually or physically disabled, mobility impaired,* etc.

See also **invalid**.

handle

As a verb, **handle** means *to manipulate with your hands* or generally *manage a situation,* Swedish **hantera**. The noun **handle** refers to *the part by which something is held, carried, or controlled,* Swedish **handtag**. The verb comes from Old English HANDLIAN and the noun from Old English HANDLE, both related to *hand*.

In Swedish, the verb **handla** has several meanings. One is *to act* and another *to do the shopping*. The word can also mean *to trade* or *do business*. Referring to a text or, for example, a film or a radio broadcast, **handla om** means *to be about.*

handling

The English word is the gerund or the present participle of the verb **handle**, Swedish **hantera**. A gerund is a verb form that functions as a noun. **His handling of the crisis** refers to *how he managed the crisis,*

Swedish **hantering**. The present participle is used to express an action that is in progress: **They are handling the matter carefully**.

The Swedish noun **handling** can mean *action* or *deed*. Referring to a book, film, or play, **handling** means *plot* or *storyline*. **Handling** is also *a document*. **Lägga till handlingarna** means *to put aside, put on file,* or *consider a matter closed*.

happy end

The use of **happy end** in Swedish is another example of Swenglish (see **after work**). The correct English form is **happy ending**, referring to the *happy conclusion* of a book, play, film, etc. The earliest example of the expression is from the early 17th century. The Swedish version might come from the message **The End** at the end of silent films to make sure that the audience would understand that the film really had come to an end. **Happy End** for **happy ending** is used also in German and Danish. **Happy End** was the title of a Swedish film 2011 about people who all have come to cross-roads in their lives. It was also the title of a study about aging in the Nordic countries 2018–2019.

Happy end in English usually has a sexual connotation referring to massage leading to an *orgasm*, in vulgar language *a handjob*.

harm

The noun **harm** means *a physical injury* and the verb *to hurt someone* or *damage something*. In Swedish, **skada** is both the noun and the verb. The word comes from German **HARM** and Old Norse **HARMR**, *grief, sorrow*.

Harm in Swedish means *indignation, resentment, vexation*. In Old Swedish, HARMBER meant *sorrow, vexation, resentment,* but also *injury*.

hat

A **hat**, as everyone knows, is *a covering for the head*, Swedish **hatt**. While the English word covers all sorts of headgear such as a cap or a beret, a Swedish **hatt** usually has a brim all around it. Of Germanic origin, the word was in Old English HÆTT and in Old Norse HOTTR, *hood*.

Hat in Swedish means *hatred*. It is a Germanic word, known from the time of the runestones, most of which date from the late Viking Age. The word probably originally referred to *prosecution, victimization*.

heat

The noun **heat** refers to *a high temperature, hot weather,* a burning *sensation in the mouth from spicy food,* or *an intensity of feeling*. In sport, a **heat** is *a preliminary round* in a race or contest. The verb **heat** means *to make or become hot,* or *to become more intense*.

Heat is of Germanic origin. In Old English, the noun was HÆTU and the verb HÆTAN.

With the same pronunciation, the Swedish adverb **hit**, also of Germanic origin, means *here* as in **Kom hit!**, *Come here!*

See also **hit**.

hefty

Hefty in English means *large and heavy* or *done with force, powerful, vigorous, violent*. **Hefty** comes from 19th century HEFT, meaning *to lift* and *weight, heaviness*.

Häftig in Swedish, from Middle Low German HEFTIG, means *rash, impetuous, vehement*, or *sudden*. In modern colloquial language, it means *exquisite, fashionable, groovy*. The similarity with English **hefty** is just a coincidence.

hem

From Old English, **hem** refers to a line that marks *the outer limit* of something, for example, the bottom *edge* of a skirt, etc., that is folded in and stitched, Swedish **fåll, kant**. Other synonyms of **hem** are *border, boundary, circumference, rim, margin*, and *perimeter*.

To **hem in** means *to enclose, restrict, confine*. The Swedish equivalent is **hämma**, *to inhibit, obstruct*, or *stop*. In Old Norse, HEMJA meant *to bridle, curb*. The origin is Proto-Germanic *HAMJAM.

If you **hem and haw** (or **hum and haw**), you *hesitate and don't know what to say*. This **hem** arguably imitates the sound of clearing your throat. The corresponding Swedish verb is **humma** (see also **hum**).

In Swedish, **hem** means *home*. English **home** and Swedish **hem** have the same Proto-Indo-European origin, a verb meaning *to settle, dwell, be home*. In Old Swedish the word meant *dwelling-place* as well as *world*.

hen

In English, **hen** is *a female bird*, especially a domestic one, Swedish **höna**. The word is of Germanic origin.

Hen has come into Swedish quite recently as a gender-neutral pronoun to replace **han/hon** in the sense of *he/she*.

high school

In the USA, **high school** refers to compulsory education, grades 9–12, preparing for college or university studies. In the UK this is called **secondary school**. In Swedish schools, this corresponds to **gymnasiet** or **gymnasieskolan** (see **gymnasium**).

A literal translation of **high school** into Swedish is **högskola**. However, this means *education on university level*. The difference between **högskola** and **universitet** in Swedish is that universities have a general right to define and manage their postgraduate education while **högskolor** must apply for examination permits for theirs.

hiss

The verb **hiss**, an imitative word from Late Middle English, means *to make a long s-sound,* and the noun **hiss** refers to that *sound*. Hissing is often done to show disapproval.

The Swedish noun **hiss** means *lift* or *elevator*. The verb **hissa** is related to English **hoist**.

hit

The verb **hit** comes from Old Norse HITTA, *to come upon, meet with,* Old English HITTAN, *to find,* and Middle English HITTEN, *to make contact with, strike.* The word has several meanings in modern English, such as *to strike, beat, touch, cause damage,* Swedish **slå, skada**. The noun **hit** refers to *striking* or *being struck*. It can also mean *a successful song or film* or, in computing, *an item of data* that matches the requirements of a search.

Swedish has imported the noun **hit** from English, but it only applies to *a successful song, film, book, etc.,* and to the computing term just mentioned.

Swedish **hitta** means *to find*. The Swedish adverb **hit** (pronounced as English **heat**) means *here* as in **Kom hit!**, *Come here!*

See also **heat**.

home office

A **home office** is *a space* in somebody's home *designated for work*, either as self-employed or for remote work for an employer.

In the UK, **the Home Office** is *the government department* responsible for domestic affairs such as law and order, immigration, and security, Swedish **inrikesministeriet**.

In Swedish, **hemmakontor** corresponds to the first sense of the English **home office** above.

house

In English, a **house** is *a home* usually with a ground floor and one or two upper storeys. A house with only a ground floor is called a **bungalow**.

In Swedish, **hus** can apply to various types of buildings and homes, such as **enfamiljshus**, *single family home*; **småhus**, *house for one or two families*; **enplanshus**, *single storey building*; **flerfamiljshus**, *block of flats, apartment building*, literally *house for several families*; **höghus**, *high-rise building*; **radhus**, *terraced house*; **hyreshus**, *tenement building*; **husbil**, *mobile home*; **husvagn**, *caravan*; **varuhus**, *department store*.

House and **hus** probably come from a Proto-Indo-European word meaning *to cover* or *hide*.

An Englishman was invited to a Swedish family, who told him they lived in the third house on the left in Skolgatan (School Street). They waited in vain for him to turn up for dinner, and when they finally got in touch, he told them that he had not seen any houses in Skolgatan – there were only buildings.

hum

Hum, from Late Middle English, is an onomatopoetic word, i.e., one that imitates a sound. **Hum** refers to *the low, continuous sound of insects* and is used as a verb and a noun, Swedish **surra** and **surr** or **surrande**. As a verb, it can mean *to sing with closed lips*, Swedish **nynna, gnola**. As a noun it also has a special technological meaning of *an unwanted low noise* in a loudspeaker, Swedish **brum**.

If you **hum and haw**, you *hesitate and don't know what to say*, Swedish **humma**.

See also **hem**.

Hum in Swedish means *idea, smattering*. **Jag har ingen hum om det** corresponds to **I've no idea about that**. This **hum** comes from Old Swedish HUMI, *obscure notion*.

The world's smallest town is called **Hum**. It is situated on the peninsula Istria in Croatia and has a little over 20 inhabitants.

humour

If you have **humour**, you are *comic or amusing* and appreciate those qualities in others. This is **humor** in Swedish.

Humour can also refer to *a state of mind, mood, temper,* Swedish **humör**. You can lose your good **humour**.

As a verb, **humour** means *to comply with a person's wishes* in order to keep him or her happy, even if those wishes are unreasonable. In Swedish this is **blidka**.

The origin of **humour** and **humör** is the Latin word HUMOR meaning *moisture, bodily fluid*. It was believed that there were four fluids that determined a person's mental disposition, blood, phlegm, yellow bile, and black bile.

husband

A **husband** is *a married man* considered in relation to his wife. The Swedish word for **husband** is **make** or **äkta man**.

In Swedish, **husbonde** means *male head of a family, patriarch,* or *master*. The origin of both the English and the Swedish word is Old Norse HÚSBÓNDI, *master of the house,* from HÚS, *house,* and BÓNDI, *occupier and tiller of the soil.* BÓNDI was the present participle of BO, *to live.* Swedish **bonde** means *farmer*.

The British record label **His Master's Voice**® was **Husbondens röst**® in Swedish.

There is another Swedish word **husband**, which refers to *a resident musical group*.

hymn

Hymn in English corresponds to **psalm** in Swedish. **Hymn** comes from Greek HYMNOS, *song in praise of a god or hero,* and usually refers to a song sung by the whole congregation in Christian worship.

Hymn in Swedish, of the same Greek origin, means *anthem*.

I

idle

The English adjective **idle** means *doing nothing, not working, avoiding work,* Swedish **sysslolös, ledig**. It also means *pointless, without effect or purpose,* Swedish **fruktlös, meningslös**.

The verb **idle** means *to spend time not doing anything,* Swedish **slösa bort tid**, and, about an engine, *to run slowly while being out of gear,* Swedish **gå på tomgång**.

Swedish **idel** means *sheer, pure,* and *nothing but.* **Jag är idel öra** corresponds to **I'm all ears**.

intern

In English, an **intern** is *a trainee* who works, often without pay, to gain experience or qualify for a position especially in medicine or teaching. Corresponding Swedish words are **praktikant** and **lärling.**

The verb **intern** means *to imprison people,* Swedish **internera**, in, for example, a military camp.

A Swedish **intern** is *an inmate in a prison*.

The word comes from Latin INTERNUS, *within, internal.*

invalid

This English word means *not valid, legally void, incorrect,* Swedish **ogiltig,** or *sickly, incapacitated by illness or injury,* Swedish **sjuklig, klen**.

In Swedish, **invalid** only means *disabled person*. The word has been replaced by other Swedish words corresponding to *disabled, physically impaired,* etc. (see **handicapped**).

The word comes from Latin IN, *not,* and VALIDUS, *strong*.

isolate

A person or a country can be **isolated**, *separated* or *set apart* from others.

You can also **isolate** something, *identify,* for example, a problem in order to deal with it.

Isolate comes from the Latin word INSULA, *island*. The English word **insulate** of the same origin means *to cover or wrap something* or provide something with material in order to prevent loss of heat, an electric shock, etc.

Swedish **isolera** means both *isolate* and *insulate*.

Insult, *to speak to someone with disrespect,* Swedish **förolämpa**, has nothing to do with **insula**. The word comes from Latin INSULTARE, *to jump or trample* on someone.

J

jack

A **jack** in English can refer to a number of things. It can be *a device for lifting heavy objects* such as a car so that a wheel can be changed, Swedish **domkraft**. A **jack** is *a figure on a playing card*, ranking below the queen, Swedish **knekt**. Another meaning of **jack** is *a socket* or *a plug at the end of a cable or cord* used to transmit signals in sound equipment, Swedish **uttag**. **Jack** is used to typify *an ordinary man* or *someone whose name is not known*. The word comes from the given name John and was used in Middle English to denote *an ordinary man* or *a young man*. It also signified *help* as in **jackhammer**, Swedish **tryckluftsborr**, and **jackknife**, Swedish **fällkniv**. In the early 18th century, **jack** was used in the sense of *worker*, as in **lumberjack**, Swedish **timmerhuggare**.

The verb **jack** means *to lift up*, Swedish **hissa upp**. Another meaning is *to steal*, from **hijack**, Swedish **kapa, råna**.

In Swedish, **jack** is *a gash*, a deep wound, or *a notch, cut,* or *dent* on a surface. It also refers to the sound equipment mentioned above, especially in the sense of *socket*.

jag

The noun **jag** is *a thorn* or *a sharp projection*, Swedish **tagg** or **hack**, and the verb **jag** means *to stab or prick*, Swedish **tanda, nagga**. The word comes from Late Middle English, possibly denoting a sudden movement.

In North American English, **jag** refers to *booze, binge, excessive drinking*, Swedish **fylla**.

Jag in Swedish corresponds to the English first-person pronoun **I**.

jest

The noun **jest** means *a joke,* something said or done for amusement, Swedish **skämt**. The verb **jest** means *to speak in a joking way*, Swedish **skämta, skoja**. The word comes from Latin GESTA, *actions, exploits*. Originally it meant *heroic deed,* and later it referred to *an idle tale, a joke*.

Jäst in Swedish means *yeast*. The word comes from Old Swedish IÆSTER, from Proto-Germanic *JESTUZ, from Proto-Indo-European *YES-, *to boil to foam*.

K

kind

The English noun **kind** refers to *a group* of people or things with similar characteristics. Synonyms are *sort, variety, type, species, category,* etc., Swedish **sort, slag**. The word has a Germanic origin, in Old English CYNDE or GECYNDE, in the sense of *nature, natural order,* and *innate character.*

Kind is also an English adjective meaning *friendly, good-natured, warm-hearted,* etc., Swedish **snäll, vänlig**. The adjective has the same origin as the noun, but in Middle English the meaning was *well born, well bred,* hence *courteous, gentle.*

If you pay **in kind**, Swedish **i natura**, the payment is in the form of *goods or services* instead of money.

The Swedish word **kind** means *cheek,* either side of the face below the eye. It comes from Old Norse KINN. Swedes may confuse **kind** with English **chin**, *the central part of the jaw* below the mouth, which is **haka** in Swedish.

kiss

As we all know, a **kiss** in English is an expression of love or affection, shown by pressing your lips onto, usually, another person's mouth or cheek. The word comes from an old English verb CYSSAN, meaning *touch with the lips*. In Swedish, the noun is **kyss** and the verb **kyssa**.

In stark contrast, the Swedish word **kiss**, originally from child language, means *pee* or *urine*.

knack

If you have a **knack** for something, you have *a skill* at doing it or you have *a tendency* to do it. The corresponding Swedish word is **talang** or **benägenhet**. In Middle English, KNACK meant *a sharp blow or sound*.

That Middle English meaning is reflected in Swedish **knack**, which means *knock* as in **Knack, knack, vem där?**, *Knock, knock, who's there?*

knot

A **knot** is made by making *a loop* on a string or rope and tightening it, Swedish **knut** or **knop**. **Knot** is also *a measure of speed*, one nautical mile per hour, Swedish **knop**.

Knot comes from Old English CNOTTA, *intertwining of ropes, cords, etc.*, of West Germanic origin.

The Swedish noun **knot**, probably of onomatopoetic origin, means *murmuring* or *grumbling*. The corresponding verb is **knota**.

Knott in Swedish is an insect, *a gnat*, Latin *Simuliidae*.

L

lag

As a verb, **lag** means *to fall behind, not keep pace*, etc., Swedish **sacka efter**. The noun **lag** means *a retardation, a period of time between two events*, Swedish **försening, fördröjning**. The word is of Scandinavian origin; LAGGA in Norwegian dialect means *to go slowly*.

Lag in Swedish is a noun. The two most common translations are *team* and *law*. Both words are related to LIGGA, English **lie**, *recline*. **Lag** is also a *decoction* or *solution*, related to the Scottish word LOCH.

lager

In English a **lager** is *a light beer*. The word comes from German LAGER, *storehouse*. Beer was brewed in the winter and then stored in caves during the summer.

The Swedish word **lager** has several meanings. One is the same as in English, referring to *a kind of beer*. From German LAGER, the word can also mean *stock, inventory*, and *warehouse*. It can also denote *a layer*. **Lager** is also a green plant, in English *lorbeer*, Latin *Laurus nobilis*.

Swedish **lager** is also a technical term, *bearing*, such as **kullager**, *a ball bearing*, used to reduce friction between machine parts.

landscape

Landscape in English is *a scenery in the countryside,* a panorama, a vista. The word also refers to *a painting of a landscape.* Another **landscape** is a format, *a horizontal image or screen* with its width larger than its height; the opposite orientation is called **portrait**.

Landskap in Swedish has the same meanings of *scenery* and *painting,* but it is also *a province.* Sweden has 25 **landskap**, some of which were independent political entities with their own laws until 1634. **Landscape** and **landskap** have the same Middle Dutch origin, LANTSCAP.

last

In English, **last** has several meanings. It can refer to *the most recent occasion* (since last Monday), *what is left after all others are gone* (his last cigarette) or *that which comes at the end* (the last chapter of the book). In Swedish, **förra** or **senaste** could be used in the first example, and **sist** or **sista** in the last two ones. **Last** comes from Middle English LASTE, a variant of LATEST.

As a verb **last** means *to continue for a certain length of time,* Swedish **vara**, or *to remain in the same condition,* Swedish **räcka, förbli**.

In Swedish, **last** means *load, burden, cargo,* or *freight,* from Germanic HLADAN-, *to pile up, pack,* but also *vice, bad habit,* from a Germanic verb LAHAN, *to blame.*

lawn

A **lawn** is *an area of grass*, usually in a park or near a house and regularly cut to keep it short, Swedish **gräsmatta**, literally *grass carpet*. The word comes from Old French LAUNDE, *wooded district, heath*.

The Swedish noun **lån** sounds the same as **lawn**, but it means *loan*, related to English **lend**. The word comes from the Germanic verb LIHWAN, *to lend*.

lax

In English, **lax** is an adjective meaning *relaxed* or *not strict enough*, from Latin LAXUS, *loose*. The Swedish equivalent is **slapp**.

A Swedish **lax** is *a salmon*, Latin *Salmo salar*. **En glad lax** is *a lively fellow*. In colloquial Swedish, **lax** refers to *a bank note for one thousand kronor*.

lecture

In Late Middle English, LECTURE meant *reading*, a text *to read*, from Latin LEGERE, *to read*. **Lecture** (which is both a verb and a noun) is used to mean *talk to an audience*, particularly to students at a university. **Lecture** can also be used to refer to a serious speech in order to *reprimand* somebody. **To lecture** is **föreläsa** in Swedish and **a lecture** is **en föreläsning**.

Lektyr in Swedish only refers to *reading matter*. It is also the name of a men's magazine.

led

Led in English is preteritum (simple past tense) and perfect participle of **lead**, a verb with several meanings. The origin is a Proto-Germanic word meaning *to cause one to go, to lead*. You can **lead** a person or an animal by your hand *to make them move forward*. You can *show somebody the way* by going in front of or beside them. To **lead** is *to be in command* or *to organize* something. You can **lead** an orchestra or a band. A door can **lead** to a corridor or a hallway, and a corridor can **lead** to a room. You **lead** by *being the first* or *having an advantage* over competitors in a game or a race. **Lead** can also *express a reason or a result*: **This will lead to a disaster. This led me to the conclusion that...** And you can **lead** (experience) a good life. **Lead** in Swedish is **leda, föra**, and **led** is **ledde, förde**.

LED is an acronym for *light emitting diode,* a semiconductor device that emits light when a current flows through it. This acronym is used in both English and Swedish.

The Swedish word **led** has several meanings. From an Old Swedish word for *journey, trip*, it can mean *way, route, direction,* or *thoroughfare*. **Led** can be *a joint, a segment, a link, a stage,* or *a part of something,* from an Indo-European root LI, *bend*. With the same origin, it can also refer to *a generation,* a degree of kindred. As an adjective, it means *bored, fed up, weary* as well as *ugly, hideous,* and *evil, nasty*.

The Swedish verb **led** is preteritum of **lida**, *to suffer, be afflicted with,* and (about time) *to pass on, draw near*.

leg

Leg refers to *a lower limb of the body* or *a support of a table or chair*, Swedish **ben**. It can also mean *a stage of a journey*, Swedish **etapp**. **Leg** comes from an Old Norse word LEGGR, which meant both *leg* and *bone of the arm or leg*. Swedish has one word, **ben**, for *leg* and *bone*.

In Swedish, **leg** is a colloquial abbreviation of the word **legitimation**, which means *identification*. So don't be surprised if you hear the question, **'Can you show your leg, please?'** in a Swedish liquor store if you look very young.

The Swedish noun **lägg** has the same pronunciation as English **leg**. **Lägg** has two meanings. It can refer to *a hand or knuckle of pork* or to *a newspaper article or file*.

Lägg! is also the imperative mood of the verb **lägga**, *to put*.

See also **bone**.

let

The main meaning of the verb **let** is *to allow* or *permit*, Swedish **låta**. It can also mean *to allow someone to use a room or a building* in return for money every week or month, Swedish **hyra ut**. Of Germanic origin, LÆTAN in Old English meant *to leave behind, leave out*.

With the same pronunciation, the Swedish adjective **lätt** is used in two senses, *light, gentle, faint,* and *easy, simple*.

lie

The English noun **lie** refers to *something you say or write that you know is untrue*, Swedish **lögn**, and the verb **lie** means *to tell someone something that is not true*, Swedish **ljuga**. The word comes from a Proto-Indo-European word meaning *to tell lies, swear, complain,* in Old English LYGE, *lie, falsehood*.

There is another English **lie**. This is a verb meaning *to recline, be in a horizontal position*, for example on a bed, Swedish **ligga**. The word can also mean *to be situated*. It has a Germanic origin from an Indo-European root, in Old English LICGAN, related to Latin LECTUS, *bed*, and German LIEGEN, *to lie*.

The Swedish noun **lie** means *scythe*. The word comes from Proto-Indo-European *LEU, to cut.

lift

The verb **lift** means *to raise to a higher position, move upwards*, Swedish **lyfta, höja**. In colloquial language it means **to steal**, Swedish **knycka, stjäla**. It can also mean *to formally remove a restriction* such as an embargo, Swedish **häva**.

The noun **lift** refers to *a device that carries people and goods up and down between floors of a building*. This is in Swedish **en hiss** and in North American English **an elevator**.

A **ski-lift** carries skiers up a slope.

To give somebody a lift means *to give them a free ride* in your car.

Lift comes from Old Norse LYPTA; it is of Germanic origin and is related to **loft**.

Lift in Swedish only refers to a *free ride* in somebody's car. The corresponding verb is **lifta**, *to hitch-hike*.

liquor

Liquor, from the same Latin word meaning *fluidity, liquid*, is *a strong alcoholic drink*, Swedish **sprit**.

Likör is Swedish for *liqueur*, a liquor with sugar and flavours and sometimes with a lower proof.

list

A **list** is *a sequence of items*, names, numbers, etc., written one below the other. The word comes from French LISTE, of Germanic origin.

List can also be a verb, meaning *to make a list*. The Swedish word for both the noun and the verb is **lista**.

The Swedish word **list** means two different things, *border, edging, strip, skirting-board*, from Old Swedish LIST, and *cunning, craftiness*, from Gothic LAIS, *I know, I have discovered*, related to **learn**, Swedish **lära**. The verb **lista ut** means *to find out*.

loan

From Old Norse LÁN, *a gift from a superior*, **loan** means *something that is borrowed*. The word is also a verb meaning *to lend*.

The Swedish verb **låna** means both *to lend* and *to borrow*. English **lend** is in Swedish also **låna ut**. Ett **lån** is *a loan*.

Native English speakers should not be surprised if a Swedish visitor asks **May I borrow your bathroom?** not knowing that the correct phrase is **May I use your bathroom?**

local

The English adjective **local** refers to a particular *area or region*. We can talk about **a local phone call**, Swedish **lokalsamtal**, or **a local train**, Swedish **lokaltåg**.

As a noun, **local** can be *an inhabitant of a particular area*, Swedish **ortsbo**. **There were more tourists than locals at the market.** In colloquial language, **a local** is *a pub* close to a person's home, Swedish **kvarterspub**.

The Swedish adjective **lokal** has the same meaning as the English one, but the noun **lokal** means *a room, premises*, or *a habitat*.

Local and **lokal** come from Latin LOCUS, *place*.

lock

Lock is of Germanic origin, related to German **LOCH**, *hole*. It was LOC in Old English. A **lock**, Swedish **lås**, is *a mechanism to keep a door, a lid, etc., fastened,* usually with a key. A **lock** on a computer or a smartphone requires a password to allow access. A **lock** is also *a short section of a canal*, Swedish **sluss**, with gates at either end to regulate the water level so that boats can be raised or lowered to the next level.

The verb **lock** means *to secure with a lock, to restrict access,* Swedish **låsa**, or *to pass through a lock on a canal*, Swedish **slussa**.

You can also talk about **a lock of hair**, *a curl,* hair that coils together. This lock is related to German **LOCKE** with the same meaning; it was LOCC in Old English.

In Swedish as in English, **lock** is *a curl or ringlet,* a *lock of hair*. However, it is also *a lid* or *cap*.

The Swedish verb **locka** has three meanings, *to call, to curl,* and *to entice or tempt*. **Med lock och pock** corresponds to **by hook or by crook** in the sense of *trying every means of persuasion*.

loo

Loo is an informal word for *toilet* in English, Swedish **dass, toa**. There are differing theories about the origin of the word. One suggestion is that it comes from **WATERLOO**, a brand name for cisterns. Another idea is that the origin was a French phrase, **GUARDEZ L'EAU**, *watch out for the water*, which became **GARDYLOO** in English. In medieval times, a servant would empty a chamber pot from an upstairs window and warn passers-by by shouting **gardyloo**. A third theory maintains that **loo** comes from French LE LIEU, *the place*. For other euphemistic words for toilet, see **restroom**.

Loo was also *a card game* in the late 1600s.

In Swedish, **lo** is *a lynx*. The origin is an Indo-European root LUK-, *shine, glow*, referring to the animal's eyes or fur. This became LOX in Old English.

lore

The English word **lore** refers to a body of *traditions* held by a particular group of people, usually **folklore**, Swedish **folklore, folkkultur**. The word is of Germanic origin, related to **learn**.

In Swedish, with the same pronunciation as **lore**, **lår** has two meanings. It is a part of the human body, *a thigh*, from an Indo-European root LEK, *to bend or be bent*. **Lår** is also *a bin* or *container*, usually a wooden one, especially one for storing firewood, from Old Swedish LAR.

luck

Luck, of West Germanic origin, refers to *success or failure by chance*. You can talk about **good luck**, Swedish **tur**, and **bad luck**, Swedish **otur**, and you can wish somebody **Good luck!**, Swedish **Lycka till!**

The Swedish word **lycka** means *happiness, bliss,* as well as *a small meadow surrounded by a forest*. The word comes from Middle Low German and shares its origin with English **luck**.

lump

A **lump** in English means *a compact mass* of a substance, usually without a regular shape, *a bulge, bump, swelling,* or *tumor*, Swedish **klump, knöl**. However, **a lump of sugar**, Swedish **sockerbit**, is usually regular.

A **lump** also refers to *an awkward, stupid person*, Swedish **tjockskalle**, literally *thickhead*.

Lump probably has a Germanic origin, a word meaning *shapeless piece*.

When you **lump things together**, you *treat them as alike, a whole*, Swedish **slå ihop**. **To lump it** means *to accept something you don't like*, Swedish **ta det som det är**.

Lump in Swedish is *old rags, thrash, junk*. The word is related to English **limp**. The adjective **lumpen** means *petty, mean, despicable*. A type of paper, **lumppapper**, is made of rags.

There is also a colloquial noun **lumpen** (definite form of *old rags*), meaning *compulsory military service*.

lure

To **lure** is *to tempt someone to do something*, usually by offering some sort of reward, Swedish **locka, fresta**. The corresponding noun is **lure**, *attraction*. **Lure** is also *a decoy*, Swedish **bete, lockbete**, a type of bait in fishing and hunting. The word comes from Old French LUERE.

In Swedish, **lura** means *to deceive, trick, cheat, swindle, delude*, from a word originally meaning *to screw up one's eyes*, related to Middle English LUREN, *to lour* or *lower*. **Lur** as a noun can refer to *a nap*, a brief sleep, or a musical instrument, *horn*. **Lur** was also *a bronze trumpet* from the Bronze Age. **Ligga på lur** means *lie in wait, lurk*.

Hörlur is in English *earphone, headphone*.

lust

This English word is both a noun and a verb. From a Proto-Indo-European word meaning *to be eager, wanton, unruly*, in Old English LUST meant *desire, appetite, pleasure*. It took on its modern meaning of *strong sexual desire* in the 1500s.

In Swedish, **lust** has two meanings, *desire* and *inclination, a wish to do something that would give pleasure or satisfaction*. In the latter meaning, Swedish **ha lust** (*have lust*) corresponds to **feel like, fancy,** or **be in the mood for** in English.

M

magazine

Magazine in English has two meanings, *a periodical publication* and *a container for ammunition in a gun* or (now obsolete) *for storing and feeding film to a camera.*

Magazine came into English from French MAGASIN, originally from Arabic MAKZIN or MAKZAN, *storehouse,* via Italian MAGAZZINO.

Magasin in Swedish has the same meanings, but in addition it also retains the old Arabic meaning of *warehouse.*

make

When you **make** something, you *create it, cause it to exist,* Swedish **göra, tillverka, skapa**. You can **make a sandwich, make a list**, and **make a wish**. When you **make your bed**, you *arrange the bedclothes* in a tidy way. You can **make a good impression**, and you can **make a decision**.

A generic Swedish translation of the verb **make** is **göra** (which also means **do**), but some English phrases with **make** are expressed in one word in Swedish. **Make your bed** is **bädda**, **make a wish** is **önska, make a knot** is **knyta**.

The English noun **make** can refer to *the trade name* or *manufacturer* of a product, Swedish **varumärke**.

Make comes from Old English MACIAN from a Proto-Germanic word meaning *fitting;* it is related to **match**.

The Swedish word **make** means *husband* or *one of a pair* (of gloves, etc.) or *match, like, peer*. It has the same Germanic origin with the sense of *fitting together*.

The female form of Swedish **make** is **maka**, *wife*. Both words are rather old-fashioned.

map

A **map**, Swedish **karta**, is *a representation of an area* showing cities, roads, islands, etc. The word comes from Latin MAPPA, *cloth*, and MAPPA MUNDI, *sheet of the world*. **Map** is also used as a verb, Swedish **kartlägga**.

The Swedish word **mapp** means *file, folder,* or *portfolio*. It has the same Latin origin.

mark

A **mark** is *a visible impression, a characteristic feature,* or *a small area* with a different colour from its surrounding. The word can also refer to *a symbol or figure* made to indicate something. As a verb, **mark** means *to make a stain* on something or *to write a word or symbol* on something to give information about, for example, ownership. The original Proto-Indo-European word meant *edge, border, boundary*. The corresponding Swedish noun is **märke** and the verb **märka** or **markera**.

Mark in Swedish means *ground, soil, land,* or *territory*. It has the same Proto-Indo-European origin.

mask

A **mask** is used to cover a face or part of a face as *a disguise* to amuse or frighten others or as *protection* against harmful substances that might be inhaled or transferred without the mask.

The verb **mask** means *to cover with a mask* or *conceal* something from view.

The Swedish noun **mask** has the same definitions as the English above. The origin is probably medieval Latin MASCA, *witch,* which became MASCHERA or MASCARA in Italian and then MASQUE in French. The word may also have been influenced by Arabic MASKARA or MASHARAT, *buffoon*.

In Swedish, **mask** also means *worm,* from a Germanic word MAð, *nibble, gnaw*.

mat

You can wipe your feet on a **mat**, also called a **door mat**, a piece of coarse material put on a floor. The Swedish word **matta** refers both to *a mat* and *a carpet*.

English **mat** and Swedish **matta** come from Latin MATTA, *mat made of rushes,* probably of Punic or Phoenician origin.

A **mat** is also a smaller piece of material put on a table to protect it from the heat of an object placed on it. The Swedish word for this is **underlägg**.

Another meaning of **mat** is *a mount for a picture*, in Swedish **passepartout** (from French). This **mat** comes from a French adjective MAT, *dull surface or finish*.

Matt in Swedish means *faint, feeble, dull, lacklustre,* and *frosted*. The word has the same origin as **matt**, *checkmate*, in a game of chess, from Arabic SCHAH MAT, *the king is dead*.

The Swedish word **mat** means *food*. The word is related to Old English **mete**, *meat*.

meaning

Meaning, Swedish **mening, betydelse,** is *what is meant* by a word, an expression, etc., in other words *a definition or explanation*. You can also give somebody **a meaning look**, Swedish **en menande blick**, when you communicate something without expressing it clearly in words.

Mean comes from Old English MÆNAN from an Indo-European word related to **mind**.

Mening in Swedish has the same, well, *meaning* or *significance* as in English, but it can also mean *a sentence* (a language unit), *an opinion*, or *an intention*. **Vad är meningen med detta?** is in English **What's the point of this?**

met

Met is the past tense and past participle of the verb **meet**, *to encounter or come together*. Swedish **möta**. **Meet** is of Germanic origin.

With the same pronunciation, Swedish **mätt** means *full, had enough to eat* related to Gothic MATJAN, *eat*. It is also past participle of the verb **mäta**, *to measure*, from an Indo-European root MED, *to measure, calculate*.

mile

Mile comes from Latin MILIA PASSUUM, meaning *one thousand paces*. As a measure of distance, it referred to the Roman mile, which was a thousand paces or double steps and measured 1 483 metres (some sources say 1 479 metres). An English mile is 1 609 metres or 5 280 feet. This **mile** is a British imperial unit and a United States customary unit. The international **nautical mile** measures 1 852 metres or 6 076 feet. It is used in air, marine, and space navigation. From this we have the unit of speed, **knot**, which is one nautical mile per hour. **Nautical mile** in Swedish is **nautisk mil** or **distansminut**, and **knot** is **knop**.

A Swedish **mil** is *ten kilometres* or 10 000 metres.

Fuel consumption of a car is measured in **mpg**, *miles per gallon*, in the UK and the USA. A US gallon is about one-fifth smaller in volume than a UK (or Imperial) gallon. An Imperial gallon is 4.546 litres, a US [liquid] gallon is about 3.785 litres.

In Sweden, fuel consumption is measured in **l/mil**, *liter per mil* or, more common nowadays, **l/100 km**, *liter per 100 kilometer*.

minute

The English noun **minute** usually refers to *a measure of time*, sixty seconds or one sixtieth of an hour. It can also be one sixtieth of a circle. The word comes from the Latin PARS MINUTA PRIMA, *first small part* (**second** comes from PARS MINUTA SECUNDA, *second small part*).

The adjective **minute** means *very small* or *detailed*, from a Latin word meaning *to diminish, make small*. The corresponding Swedish words are **minimal** and **detaljerad**.

Minutes are the written record of a meeting. This is **protokoll** in Swedish.

In Swedish, **minut** only refers to *sixty seconds* or *one sixtieth of a circle*, but **sälja (köpa) i minut** is *to sell (buy) by retail*.

mitten

Mittens keep your hands warm in cold weather. A **mitten**, Swedish **vante**, has one compartment for the thumb and one for the rest of the fingers. Boxing gloves are sometimes called **mittens**, Swedish **boxhandskar**. Originally, **mitten** was *a silk glove for women* covering the forearm, the wrist, and part of the hand. **Mitten** comes from an Old French word MITAIN, possibly from MITE, a playful *name for a cat*, or alternatively, from a Proto-Indo-European word meaning *between, in the middle*.

In Swedish, **mitten** means *the middle*, from Latin MEDIUS, *in the middle*.

mob

A **mob** is *a large, noisy crowd,* particularly one that is angry or violent, in Swedish **pöbel, folkhop**. In the USA a **mob** is *a criminal gang*. The verb **mob** means *to form a crowd around a celebrity* in order to express admiration or attack them. **Mob** comes from Latin MOBILE VULGUS, *excitable crowd*.

From English, the Swedish verb **mobba** means *to bully* someone; the person who does so is **en mobbare**.

moot

To moot something is *to suggest it for discussion,* and **a moot point** is *a subject about which different people have different opinions*.

The Swedish preposition **mot** means *against* or *towards*. **Mot** is also a noun referring to *a [motorway] junction* from an Old Swedish word meaning *meeting*.

Moot and **mot** have the same Germanic origin related to English **meet**.

motion

In English, **motion** is the process of *moving or being moved,* Swedish **rörelse**. A **motion** is also *a formal proposal* to bring something up for discussion at a meeting or in Parliament. **Motion** is also used as a verb, *to propose for discussion and resolution*. The verb can also mean *to direct or give* *somebody a sign* to do something. The word comes from the Latin noun MOTIO from the verb MOVERE, *to move*.

In Swedish, **motion** refers to *physical exercise*. It also shares the meaning of *proposal* with the English noun when a member of the Swedish Parliament proposes something. If the government introduces a bill, it is called **proposition** from Latin PROPONERE, *to put forth, set forth, display*.

See also **proposition**.

mundane

Mundane in English means *dull, boring, worldly*. It comes from Latin MUNDUS, *world*. The Swedish equivalent is **banal**.

The Swedish word **mondän** means *elegant, fashionable, sophisticated*, from French MONDAINE, *elegant*.

murder

A **murder**, from an Indo-European word meaning *death*, is a crime, a *premeditated killing* of somebody, in Swedish **mord**. The person who commits a murder is a **murderer,** Swedish **mördare**.

The English ending -**er** in **murder** may lead Swedish speakers to wrongly think that the word means **mördare**. (See also **photograph**).

must not

In English, **must not** tells you that you are *forbidden* to do something.
Måste inte in Swedish means *don't have to*, which may lead Swedes to think that **must not** is not very strict, just a recommendation. **Don't have to** in English implies that *it is not necessary* to do something.

N

nature

From Latin NATUS, *born*, **nature** refers to *that which is not controlled by humans*, such as animals and plants, weather, etc., Swedish **naturen**. **Nature** is sometimes personified, written with a capital **N** or as **Mother Nature**. **Nature** also denotes *character, type, personality,* or *temperament*. This is also **natur** in Swedish.

When your Swedish friends talk about **the beauty of the Swedish nature**, they do not refer to any Swedish national character but the Swedish *countryside, scenery,* or *landscape*. And if they tell you how much they like to be **out in the nature**, they simply want to say that they like to be *in the countryside*.

necessary

Necessary, from Latin NECESSE, *to be needful*, means *essential* or *inevitable*. The corresponding Swedish word is **nödvändig**.

The Swedish noun **necessär** from French NÉCESSAIRE, *necessary*, means *toilet bag, washbag*, arguably an essential component of your luggage.

neck

Neck is *the body part that connects the head to the rest of the body*. It is also *the part of a garment* that goes round the neck. The word is also used for *a narrow part* of, for example, a bottle or a guitar, violin, etc. **Neck** is in Swedish **hals** (which is also the same as the Swedish word for **throat**).

If competitors are *level in a race* and have an equal chance of winning, they are **neck and neck**, Swedish **jämsides, sida vid sida**.

Neck is also a colloquial verb describing what two persons do when they *kiss and caress amorously*, Swedish **hångla**.

Nacke is the Swedish word for *nape, back of the neck*, which Old English HNECCA also meant. **Neck** and **nacke** are of Germanic origin.

novel

Novel comes from Latin NOVUS and Italian NOVELLA, *new*. A **novel** denotes a *long, fictitious prose story*, usually divided into several chapters. In the early 16th century, a **novel** was a *short story or fable*. The Swedish word for **novel** is **roman**, whose origin is a Middle Latin word meaning *in the way of the Romans*, referring to a story written not in Latin but in a vernacular language.

The English adjective **novel**, Swedish **ny, nymodig**, means *new* or *unusual*. It comes from Latin NOVUS, *new*.

A Swedish **novell**, of the same Latin origin, is *a short story*.

O

oar

An **oar** is *a pole with a flat blade,* used to row a boat, Swedish **åra**. **Oar** is of Germanic origin; in Old English it was AR.

With roughly the same pronunciation as **oar**, Swedish **år** means *year*. **År** comes from Proto Germanic *JÆRAM, which became **year** in English and **Jahr** in German. The Greek word HORA, *year, hour,* became **hour** in English.

obligation

Obligation in English means *duty, responsibility, liability.* The corresponding Swedish word is **förpliktelse** or **skyldighet**.

The Swedish word **obligation** means *a bond,* a loan to a company or a government. The word comes via Latin and Old French from a Proto-Indo-European word meaning *to bind.*

objective

Objective in English has mainly two meanings. As an adjective it means *unbiased, impartial, disinterested,* Swedish **opartisk**. As a noun it means *aim, intention, goal, object,* Swedish **syfte**. The word was formed from

Medieval Latin OBJECTUM, *thing presented to the mind*. The meaning of *unbiased* came from German in the 1850s.

The Swedish adjective **objektiv** has the same meanings as the English adjective.

As a noun, Swedish **objektiv** means *lens*. There are various types of camera lenses, such as **teleobjektiv**, *tele lens*; **vidvinkelobjektiv**, *wide angle lens*; **zoomobjektiv**, *zoom lens*; **porträttobjektiv**, *portrait lens*.

occupation

This word originally came via Latin from a Proto-Indo-European verb, *to seize, grab*. It has several meanings in English: *job* or *profession*; *a way of spending time*; *taking control of a building, a territory or a country*; *using or living in a building*.

Swedish **ockupation** has only the meaning of *illegally seizing or taking over*.

offensive

The English adjective **offensive** and the Swedish **offensiv** both mean *aggressive, attacking*, from Latin OFFENDERE, *to displease, annoy*. As nouns, the two words can refer to *a campaign*, either a military one or one organized to achieve a political or social aim.

Contrary to Swedish **offensiv**, **offensive** in English also means *disgusting, repulsive, unpleasant, causing somebody to feel upset or annoyed*.

offer

To **offer** in English is *to present something* for somebody to accept or reject. The noun refers to *what you present* and can also mean a *specially reduced price*. The Swedish verb is **erbjuda** and the noun **erbjudande** or, in business jargon, **offert**.

Offer comes from Latin OFFERRE, *to bestow, present,* via French OFFRIR (verb) and OFFRE (noun).

The Swedish noun **offer** means *victim, prey, casualty,* or *sacrifice*.

or

Or is a conjunction, a word used to connect words or clauses or to link alternatives, as in this example: **Does the course start on Monday or Tuesday?** Or is a short form of Middle English OTHER.

The Swedish noun **or**, pronounced with a long **o** roughly as in English **too**, is a *mite*, a very small arachnid, Latin *Acarus*.

For the Swedish word **år**, which is pronounced as **or**, see **oar** above.

ordinary

Ordinary means *normal, common, standard,* or *commonplace*. The corresponding Swedish word is **vanlig, ordinär**.

Ordinarie in Swedish means *regular* or *permanent*, usually referring to a job position.

The word has a Latin origin, ORDINARIUS, *in due order*.

ore

Ore is a mineral from which metal can be obtained, Swedish **malm**. **Ore** is of West Germanic origin, related to Latin AES, *crude metal, bronze*.

For the Swedish word **år**, which is pronounced as **ore**, see **Oar** above.

outstanding

Something that is **outstanding** is *exceptionally good*; it stands out from everything else, Swedish **enastående, framstående**. **Outstanding** can also refer to a sum of money that *has not yet been paid*, Swedish **obetald, utestående**, or something that *has not yet been dealt with*, Swedish **olöst**.

A literal translation into Swedish would be **utstående**, which means *protruding* and is mostly used about a person's ears, teeth, or skin tags.

overcast

In English, **overcast** is used to describe the sky and means *cloudy, sunless, grey*, Swedish **mulen**. In the early 1300s, the verb **overcast** meant *to place something over or across*.

Swedish **överkast** has retained the Middle English sense; it means *bedspread*. **Överkast** comes from two words, *over* or *across* and *a throw*.

oversee

Oversee, from Old English OFERSEON, *to look at from above*, means *to supervise* or *monitor*, Swedish **övervaka**.

The Swedish word **överse** means *to condone, overlook, be indulgent*.

overtake

If you *catch up with and pass* another vehicle while driving, you **overtake** it, Swedish **köra om**. Relating to misfortune or a feeling, the word can also mean *come suddenly or unexpectedly*, Swedish **överraska, drabba, överväldiga**.

Överta in Swedish means *to take over* or *replace, to succeed to* someone.

P

pack up

In English, **pack up** means *to put something in a bag, a suitcase, etc.,* for travelling. It can also mean *to quit or stop doing something.*

Pack comes from Middle Dutch PAC, PACK, *bundle*, in connection with trade. English wool was exported to the Low Countries in packs.

In Swedish, **packa upp** is the opposite of **pack up**, corresponding to **unpack** in English. That is what you do when you come home from a trip. **Pack up** in Swedish is **packa** or **packa ner** (literally *pack down*). See also **button up**.

The Swedish noun **pack** is a derogatory word meaning *riffraff, rabble.*

pall

A **pall** is *a cloth spread over a coffin* at a funeral, Swedish **bårtäcke**. The word can also refer to *a dark cloud of smoke* or *something that is causing a feeling of sadness*, Swedish **slöja, hölje**. The word comes from Latin PALLIUM, *covering, cloak*, via Old English PÆLL, *cloth cover for a chalice.*

As a verb, **pall** means *to become less interesting*, Swedish **förlora dragningskraft**. The word is from Late Middle English as a shortening of APPAL.

Pall in Swedish is *a stool* or *a pallet*. The word is related to Old English PEALL, *ledge, plateau*. The colloquial Swedish verb **palla** has two meanings, *to scrump apples* and *to cope with something*.

pant

To **pant** is *to breathe quickly* or *to say something while panting*, Swedish **flämta, flåsa**. As a noun, the word means *a short, quick breath*, Swedish **flämtning**. The word is based on a Greek word PHANTASIOUN, *to cause to imagine*, from PHANTASIA, via Old French PANTASIER, *to be agitated, gasp*.

Pants in British English are *underwear, knickers, panties*, Swedish **trosor** for women's underwear and **kalsonger** for men's. The American English word **pants** refers to *trousers*, Swedish **byxor**. The word comes from PANTALOONS, originally from the Italian name PANTALONE, a commedia dell'arte figure with long trousers. (See also **trousers**.)

Swedish **pant** is *a pledge, forfeit*, or *pawn*. **Pant** is also *the deposit* you pay when you buy bottles or cans of drinks. The verb **panta** means to bring back those bottles or cans, usually by putting them into a deposit automat that will give you a ticket to redeem in the shop where you left the bottles or cans. The origin of the word is Old High German PFANT, in modern German **Pfand**.

paragraph

A **paragraph** is *a section of a text*, indicated by a new line or an indentation. The Swedish word is **stycke**.

From Greek PARA, *beside* and GRAPHEIN, *to write,* the word PARAGRAPHOS meant *short stroke marking a break in sense.*

The Swedish word **paragraf** means *section or clause in a contract, in a law text, or in the minutes of a meeting,* usually indicated by the § sign. The section sign § comes from Latin **signum sectiones**, a *sign between sections.* It is mainly used to refer to a numbered section of a document.

passe-partout

This French word meaning *pass everywhere* is used in English to denote *a master key, passkey,* or *skeleton key.* It can also refer to *a mat,* a method of framing pictures.

In Swedish, **passepartout** only means a *piece of cardboard used to frame a picture.*

patron

In English a **patron** is *someone who helps* a person, an organization, or a cause, Swedish **mecenat, gynnare**. A **patron** can also be *a client* or *customer* who regularly visits a pub, a shop, etc., Swedish **stamgäst**.

In Swedish, **patron** has two meanings. It can be *a cartridge* for a gun. And it can (or could, since this use is old-fashioned) refer to *a landlord, a country squire, a foundry proprietor,* or *a paper mill owner.*

Patron comes from Latin PATRONUS, *defender, protector of clients.*

peak

A **peak** is a *pointed shape*, particularly *a mountain top*. Figuratively, it can mean *the highest point of an achievement, activity, or quality*. As a verb, it means *to reach the highest point*. From Late Middle English it was probably a variant of PIKE, a historical *weapon* with a pointed head. **Peak** is in Swedish **topp**.

A Swedish **pik** is *a pointed weapon*. It is also *an innuendo, sneer*, or *gibe, a mean comment*, from French PIQUE, *grudge, rancour*.

See also **pike**.

personal

Personal is an adjective referring to *what belongs to or concerns a particular person* or their life. The corresponding word in Swedish is **personlig**. PERSONALIS in Latin meant *of a person*.

Personal is the Swedish noun for *personnel* or *staff*.

perverse

The English **perverse** means *unreasonable, uncooperative, obstructive, troublesome, annoying, irrational*, Swedish **motsträvig, förhärdad**.

The Swedish adjective **pervers** means *sexually deviant, kinky*. A person of that character is in English a **pervert**.

The word comes from Latin PERVERSUS, *turned about, turned upside down,* which in Middle English took on the sense of *turned about from what is right or good.*

photograph

A **photograph** is *a picture* made by a camera or, nowadays, also by a cellphone. The word is also a verb, meaning *to take a photograph*. The corresponding Swedish noun is **fotografi** or **foto**; the verb is **fotografera**.

Fotograf in Swedish means *photographer*. For possible confusion caused by nouns ending in **-er** in English, see **murder** above.

The original is two Greek words, PHOS, *light,* and GRAPHÊ, *drawing* or *writing*. When you take a photograph, you write with light.

physician

A **physician** is *a Doctor of Medicine*, especially one who specializes in diagnosis and medical treatment, in Swedish **läkare**.

The Swedish word **fysiker** means *physicist*, a student of or expert in physics.

The Latin word PHYSICA meant *relating to nature*.

pick

Pick is a verb meaning *to take or choose somebody or something*. The Swedish word is **plocka, välja**. You can **pick flowers or strawberries**, you can **pick a career**, and you can **pick out somebody in a crowd**. If you **pick pockets**, you *steal from people's pockets*. The word comes from Middle English PIKE.

The noun **pick** refers to a tool used to break up hard ground or rock, Swedish **[spets]hacka**.

Pick in Swedish is a colloquial word for *penis*. The word comes from a Germanic root meaning *being pointed*. **Pick och pack** is *bag and baggage* or *goods and chattels*.

pig

Pig is a *farm animal* (Swedish **gris** or **svin**), kept for its meat, pork. A **pig** can also refer to *a dirty or generally unpleasant person*. **Pig** probably comes from the first part of Old English PICBRED, *acorn*, literally *pig bread*.

The Swedish noun **pigg** means *spike* or *thorn*. As an adjective, **pigg** means *alert, keen, brisk, lively*. The word is related to English **pike**.

pike

A **pike** is a *long freshwater fish*, Latin *Esox lucius*, Swedish **gädda**. Because of its long, pointed jaw, it has its English name from another **pike**, an infantry weapon with a pointed head on a long wooden shaft, Swedish **pik**. The word comes from Dutch PIEK or PIKE, *pointed implement*, via French PIQUE.

Pike is also *a position in gymnastics and diving*, Swedish **pik**.

Pike is American English for **turnpike**, *a motorway on which a toll is charged*, Swedish **motorväg, betalväg**.

In addition to the reference to a weapon, Swedish **pik** also means *gibe, innuendo, sneer, a mean comment*, from French PIQUE, *grudge, rancour*.

See also **peak**.

pin

A **pin** is *a thin piece of metal with a sharp point at one end,* Swedish **nål**, used for fastening, for example, a piece of paper on a board or for sewing. The verb **pin** means *to attach or fasten with a pin* or *to hold somebody firmly so that they cannot move*. Latin PINNA meant *point, tip, edge*.

Pinne in Swedish is *a stick*. The origin is probably the same as that of **pin**.

Pin (with a long **i**) appears in a few expressions in Swedish. **På pin kiv** means *out of pure cussedness, just to tease*. **Vill man vara fin får man lida pin** means *If you want to look good, you will have to go through a great deal* or *you will have to suffer for your appearance*.

The Swedish noun **pina** means *pain, anguish, torment*, and the verb **pina** means *to torture, harass*. The word comes from Latin POENA, *punishment*, and is, of course, related to English **pain**.

pink

Pink is a colour between red and white, Swedish **skär, rosa**. The word comes from a flower in the *Dianthus* family.

Pinka in Swedish is a colloquial verb corresponding to English *to pee* or *piddle*. The word is from children's language, related to **kissa** and **pissa** of the same meaning.

pit

English **pit**, from Latin PUTEUS, *trench, pit, well*, means *a hole in the ground*, Swedish **grop**, and *a mine*, Swedish **gruva**. In motor racing, the **pit** is an area used for refuelling, tyre change, and repairing the cars during a race. In Swedish, this is called **depå**.

A **pit** is also *a seed, stone,* or *pip* inside a fruit, Swedish **kärna**. This **pit** comes from Proto-Germanic *PITTAN via Dutch PIT, *kernel, core*.

Pitt in Swedish is a mildly vulgar word for *penis*, possibly related to Middle High German PINT and Old English PINTLE.

plague

A **plague** is *an epidemic disease* with a high rate of mortality, Swedish **pest**. The noun **plague** can also refer to an extremely large number of, for example, *insects causing damage* or *a cause of irritation*, Swedish **plågoris**.

As a verb, **plague** means *to cause worry or distress* or *to persistently annoy*, Swedish **hemsöka, besvära**.

Plague comes from Latin PLAGA, *stroke, wound*.

Swedish **plåga** is both a verb, *to torment, harass*, and a noun, *pain, torment, nuisance, affliction*. It has the same Latin origin.

plug

A **plug** is *a piece of material that fits into a hole* and blocks it up, Swedish **plugg**. A **plug** can *keep water in a basin or bathtub*, Swedish **propp**. It is also *a device for connecting a mains outlet* with an electric appliance, Swedish **propp**. The verb **plug** means *to insert something into an opening* to fill it or block it, Swedish **plugga igen**. You can also **plug** something by mentioning it publicly in order *to promote* it, Swedish **göra reklam för**.

Plug comes from Middle Dutch and Middle Low German PLUGGE.

In colloquial Swedish, **plugg** means *school* or *tedious study*, and the verb **plugga** means *to study hard*. In Swedish slang, **plugg** refers to *potatoes*.

See also **prop**.

plump

This English adjective means *round, fat, chubby*, in Swedish **knubbig, rund**. As a verb, it means *to shake a pillow or cushion* so that it becomes rounded and soft, Swedish **skaka upp**. It can also mean *to sit down heavily*, Swedish **dimpa ner**.

In Swedish, the noun **plump** means *a blot*. As an adjective referring to a person, it means *coarse, forthright, raw, scurrilous*, or *ribald*.

Plump comes from Middle Dutch PLOMP, *blunt, obtuse*. This is what the word meant also in English in the late 15th century.

pocketbook

Mainly in American English, **pocketbook** means *handbag, wallet*, or *purse*, neither of which is a real book. However, the original **pocketbook** was really a book, a case with a small notepad. In British English, **pocketbook** still means *notebook*. The Swedish noun **plånbok** also meant *notepad*, but now it means *wallet*. **Utplåna**, in archaic Swedish **plåna ut**, means *delete*, from Latin PLANARE, *level out*. The original **pocketbooks** had pages of ivory or parchment that allowed written text to be deleted or erased.

The Swedish word **pocketbok**, or simply **pocket**, refers to *a book* that is small enough to fit in a pocket. The English equivalent is **paperback**, in US English also **pocket book**.

port

A **port** is *a town or city with a harbour*, Swedish **hamn, hamnstad**. Latin PORTUS meant *haven* or *harbour*.

On a ship, **port** is used in two senses. It refers to *an opening in the side* for boarding or loading goods, Swedish **lastport**. **Port** is also *the left side of the ship*, Swedish **babord**; the right side is called **starboard**, Swedish **styrbord**. This **port** comes from Latin PORTA, *gate*.

Port is also *a strong dessert wine*, originally from Portugal, Swedish **portvin**.

In Swedish, **port** refers to *a front door, gate,* or *gateway*. The colloquial verb **porta** means *to refuse a person admittance, prevent someone from entering*.

positive

This adjective means *affirmative, promising, optimistic, confident,* etc. It also means *certain, definite, absolute,* and *having an electric charge.* A **positive number** is *greater than zero*. If a test is **positive**, it *shows the presence of a certain substance or condition*.

Swedish **positiv** shares most of those meanings, but not that of *absolute, certain, definite*. The Swedish noun **positiv** is a *barrel-organ*.

Positive and **positiv** come from Latin POSITIVUS, referring to laws as being *laid down, admitting no question*.

pregnant

A woman or a female animal *expecting a child or young* is **pregnant**. The word probably comes from Latin PRAE-, *before*, and GNASCI, *to be born*. The corresponding Swedish word is **gravid**, from Latin GRAVIS, *heavy*.

Pregnant can also mean *significant, full of meaning, concise.*

Pregnant in Swedish has the latter English meaning only.

prescribe

A medicine or a treatment can be **prescribed**, *authorized*, Swedish **ordinerad**, by a doctor. **Prescribe** can also mean *to stipulate* or *impose*, Swedish **föreskriva, ålägga**.

Preskriberad in Swedish means *statute-barred*, no longer legally enforceable because the period for limitation has expired.

This word comes from Latin PRAESCRIBERE, *to direct in writing.*

present

With the stress on the first syllable, **present** in English means *existing or occurring here and now*, Swedish **närvarande** and **nuvarande**, respectively. **The present** means *the period of time just now*. The original Latin PRAESENT- meant *being at hand*.

With the same stress, the noun **present** is *a gift*. As a verb, *to formally give*, or *to introduce*, the word has the stress on the last syllable. This **present** comes from Latin PRAESENTARE, *to place before.*

The noun **present** in Swedish only refers to *a gift*. Unlike the English noun, the word has its stress on the last syllable. **Presens** in Swedish refers to *the present tense* of verbs.

present oneself

When you **present yourself**, you *talk and behave in a particular way* in front of other people, Swedish **visa upp sig**. The verb can also mean *to appear at a certain time and place*, Swedish **infinna sig**.

When a Swede says, **'Let me present myself'**, he or she really wants to say, **'Let me introduce myself'**. **Presentera sig** in Swedish means *to introduce oneself*.

presumptive

In English, **presumptive** means *presumed in lack of further information, hypothetical, speculative, likely to be true*, Swedish **sannolik, hypotetisk**. The word comes from Latin PRAESUMERE, *to presume*.

Presumtiv in Swedish (of the same Latin origin) means *prospective, possible*, or *supposed*.

price/prize

The **price** is *what you pay* for goods or services or to achieve an objective. The word is also a verb, *to decide the price of something*. **Price** comes from Latin PRETIUM, which means both *value* and *reward*.

A **prize** is *something given* to the winner of a competition or as *a reward* for an outstanding achievement. **Prize** comes from the stem of Old French PREISIER *to praise, appraise*. A **prize** is (or used to be) *an enemy ship that was* *captured* during a war. To **prize** something is *to value it very highly*, Swedish **värdera, skatta högt**, or *to use force to open something*, Swedish **bända upp**.

Price and **prize** are both **pris** in Swedish, and Swedish speakers may have problems with the distinction. **En pris snus** is *a pinch of snuff*.

prick

This English word can be a verb, *to sting* or *pierce*, Swedish **sticka, stinga**, or a noun, *a [physical or mental] pain*, Swedish **sting** or **styng**. The corresponding noun is also a vulgar word for *a penis*, Swedish **pick, pitt, kuk**. A **prick** can refer to *a stupid or contemptible man*, Swedish **idiot, skitstövel**. Prick is probably of West Germanic origin. In Old English the verb was PRICIAN and the noun PRICCA.

In Swedish, **prick** is *a dot* or *spot*. It is also *a navigation mark* at sea. In sport, a **prick** is *a penalty point*. Time for an appointment **prick klockan åtta** is *at eight o'clock sharp*. **En prick på horisonten** is *a dot on the horizon*. **Prick** corresponds to *the bull's eye* in the game of darts, and **mitt i prick** is *right on target*. **En trevlig prick**, a colloquial expression, means a *nice guy*, quite the opposite of an English **prick**.

principal

The adjective **principal** means *the first in order of importance*, Swedish **främsta, viktigaste**. The noun **principal** can refer to *the leading player* in each section of an orchestra or *the leading performer* in a concert or play. In finance, **principal** is *a sum of money invested or lent* with the aim of receiving interest, Swedish **kapital**. Especially in the USA and Australia, a **principal** is *the head of a school or college*, Swedish **rektor**. **Principal** comes from Latin PRINCEPS, *first, chief*.

The Swedish noun **principal** means *employer*; it is rather old-fashioned.

profile

A **profile** is *an outline, especially of a person's face, seen from the side*. A **profile** is also *information about or a description of somebody*. As a verb, it means *to describe somebody*.

The Swedish noun **profil** has the same meanings as the English one.

Recently, Swedish media have begun to refer to *a suspect who has been arrested for a crime* as a **profil** with a prefix such as **sportprofilen** or **kulturprofilen**. Swedish media do not usually publish the names of suspected criminals—otherwise they might be prosecuted for slander or defamation.

Profile and **profil** come from Italian PROFILARE, from PRO- *forth*, and FILARE, *to spin, to draw a line*. FILUM in Latin meant a *thread*.

prognosis

Prognosis in English usually refers to *the likely course of a medical condition*. The Greek origin of the word meant *foreknowledge, perceiving beforehand*.

Also in Swedish, **prognos** is used about a medical condition, but in addition it means *forecast* about the weather, the outcome of an election, or (in business) future sales. The word can also mean *prediction*.

prop

The English noun **prop**, probably from Middle Dutch and Middle Low German PROPPE, *support for a vine,* and *stopper for a bottle,* refers to something that *supports* something else or *keeps it in position,* Swedish **stöd**. The corresponding verb is **prop**, Swedish **stötta**.

Props are objects that are used in a play or film, Swedish **rekvisita**. The word is an abbreviation of **properties**.

Mainly in American slang, **props** means *credit, recognition,* or *respect*.

With the same origin as the English noun, the Swedish noun **propp** means *plug, stopper,* and *electrical plug, fuse.* **Blodpropp** means *blood clot* or *embolism*.

In the 1860s, Swedish forestry began exporting **pitprops** to coal mines in the UK, and the word was included in the Swedish language. The export grew, and in 1873, more than 15 million pitprops were exported. Coal had long been used for heating and for forging in the UK, but when steam began to be used in industry and for railway transport, coal production increased and the need for pitprops grew dramatically.

See also **plug**.

proper

In English, a **proper** job is *a real* job. **Proper** can also mean *appropriate, suitable*. English **proper** is **riktig, lämplig, passande** in Swedish.

Proper comes from Latin PROPRIUS, *one's own, special*.

Of the same origin, Swedish **proper** means *tidy, neat*, or *decent*.

proposition

In English, a **proposition** is *something presented to somebody for consideration*, Swedish **förslag**. It can also be a *statement* to be discussed or explained or *something that somebody intends to do*.

The verb **proposition** means *to suggest to somebody, often in an offensive way, to have sex*, Swedish **göra ett skamligt förslag**.

The Swedish word **proposition** means *a government bill*, a bill introduced to Parliament by the government. When a member of the Swedish Parliament proposes something, it is called a **motion**.

Proposition comes from the Latin verb PROPONERE, *to set forth*.

prospect

In English, **prospect** means *the likelihood of something happening* in the future, Swedish **utsikt, möjlighet**. The word also means a person that is *a* *potential future client or customer*, Swedish **möjlig kund**. As a verb, **prospect** means *to search for minerals* such as copper or gold, Swedish **prospektera**.

Prospect comes from a Latin verb PROSPICERE, *to look forward*.

The Swedish word **prospekt** means *prospectus, leaflet, brochure*.

protocol

The English word means *a code of behaviour* in a group or organization. PROTOCOLE was the forms of etiquette to be observed by the French head of state in the 19th century. **Protocol** can also refer to *the terms of a treaty*. In science, the word relates to *how to carry out* an experiment or a medical treatment. In computing, it means a set of rules governing *the exchange of data between devices*. The word comes from Greek PROTOKOLLON, meaning *that which is glued first*. The first page of a roll of papyrus showed the table of contents.

The Swedish word **protokoll** has the same origin as the English one and shares the meaning of code of behaviour and the computing term, but its most common meaning is *the minutes* or *records* of a meeting.

provision

Provision, from Latin PROVIDERE, *to foresee, attend to*, refers to the action of *providing something* or *that which is provided*, such as food and drink for a journey or an amount of money set aside from profits for future bad debts. The Swedish for this is **försörjning** or **proviant**; the financial word is **avskrivning**. **Provision** is also used to express *a condition or requirement* in, for example, a legal document. This **provision** is in Swedish **villkor** or **stadga**.

In Swedish, **provision**, of the same Latin origin, means *commission*, that is, a sum of money paid to an agent.

public

The Latin word PUBLICUS meant *of the people, common* (it was a combination of POPLICUS, *of the people*, and PUBES, *adult*). In English, **public** means *general, common, open, not private*, Swedish **offentlig** or **allmän**. Therefore, it seems strange that a **public school** in England and Wales is an older private, fee-charging school, Swedish **privatskola**.

Among the most famous **public schools** are Eton, Harrow, Rugby, and Winchester. They are called **public schools** because they are open to pupils irrespective of where they live or their religion.

In Scotland as in the USA, **public schools** are state schools.

In the UK, a **public** is short for *public bar* or *public house*, most often shortened to **pub**.

The public refers to *people in general, the community*, in Swedish **allmänheten**.

The Swedish noun **publik** means *audience*. There is also an adjective **publik**, which is mainly used about *companies listed on a stock exchange*, **publika företag**.

pus

Pus comes from Latin PUS, *matter from a sore,* and that is exactly what it is, dead white blood cells and dead bacteria, usually found where there is an infection. The Swedish word for this is **var**.

The Swedish word **puss** has two very different meanings, a *puddle* and a *brief or light kiss*. A loving couple will often end a telephone conversation by saying **puss, puss**, meaning *I love you*. This **puss** is most likely onomatopoetic.

R

rabbit

A **rabbit** is a mammal with long ears, long hind legs, and a short tail, Latin *Oryctolagus cuniculus*, Swedish **kanin**. **Rabbit** probably comes from Old French and may be of Dutch origin.

The Swedish word **rabatt** has two meanings. One is *discount* or *rebate*, from Anglo-Norman French REBATRE, *to beat back, deduct*. The other is *flowerbed*, from French RABAT, *foldable collar*, from REBATTRE, *to turn down, fold*.

See also **rebate**.

rank

A **rank** is *a position* in the hierarchy of society, the armed forces, an organization, or in statistics, Swedish **rang**. A **rank** is also *a row or line* of things or people, such as soldiers or police officers, Swedish **led**.

The verb **rank** means *to place someone or something in a grading system*, Swedish **rangordna**.

Rank is of Germanic origin, from Old French RANC.

The adjective **rank** refers to *vegetation growing too thickly*, Swedish **frodig, övervuxen**. It can also mean *smelling unpleasant*, Swedish **illaluktande**. RANC in Old English meant *proud, rebellious*.

The Swedish adjective **rank** is mainly used about small boats and means *unsteady*. Referring to a person, **rank** means *tall and slender*. The word is of Germanic origin.

rapport

In English, **rapport** refers to *a good understanding* or *a harmonious relationship* between people and *an ability to communicate well*. A lecturer wants to have a good **rapport** with his or her audience. In Swedish this would be **en bra relation** or **bra publikkontakt**. This sense of the word emerged in the mid 17th century. In Middle English the word meant *report* or *talk*, from French RAPPORTER, *to bring back*.

The Swedish word **rapport** means *report* and has the same French origin. The news on one Swedish TV channel is called **Rapport**, on another it is called **Aktuellt** (see **actual**).

rare

One sense of **rare** is *not occurring very often*, synonymous with *infrequent* and *scarce*, Swedish **sällsynt**. When something is not found in large numbers, it is **rare** and often also *of more interest or value*. **Rare** can also mean *remarkable, unusually good*, Swedish **enastående**. From Latin RARUS, *thinly sown*, the Late Middle English word RARE meant *widely spaced, infrequent*.

In cooking, **rare** refers to meat that is *lightly cooked*, so that the inside is red, Swedish **lättstekt, blodig**. In this sense, the word comes from Old English REAR, which meant *half-cooked* and used to refer to soft-boiled eggs.

The Swedish word **rar** does have the meaning of *infrequent*, but as such it is mostly used about seldom found books or endangered species, animals or plants threatened with extinction. A more common sense of **rar** in Swedish is *gentle, kind, sweet, endearing, lovely, charming*. Danish **rar** has the same meaning, but in Norwegian, **rar** mainly means *odd, peculiar, eccentric, strange*. This is logical, since what we seldom meet may seem strange to us.

rate

A **rate** in English is *a fixed price* for something bought or rented, in Swedish **pris** or **kostnad**. **Rate** also refers to an amount expressed as *a percentage of another amount*, such as **interest rate**, Swedish **ränta**. In the UK, a **rate** is *a local tax* on commercial land and buildings, in Swedish **taxa** or **tariff**. **Rate** is also *speed, frequency, quantity*, etc., especially compared with another quantity or measure. Corresponding Swedish words would be **fart, takt, grad, mått,** or **frekvens**.

The verb **rate** means *to estimate* or *assign a value to something*, Swedish **värdera** or **uppskatta**.

Rate comes from Latin RATUS, *reckoned*.

The Swedish verb **rata** means *to reject, refuse,* or *turn down* something because it is distasteful or useless, possibly from a Norwegian word RÄT meaning *rubbish, waste*.

rebate

If you have paid too much for tax, rent, or a utility, you may get *a refund*, a **rebate**, Swedish **återbäring, avdrag**. Another sense of **rebate** is *a deduction* or *discount*. The word comes from Anglo-Norman French REBATRE, *to beat back, deduct*.

Rabatt in Swedish means *discount* or *reduction*, of the same origin as **rebate**. It also means *flower bed*. In this sense, the word comes from French RABAT, *foldable collar*, from RABATTRE, *to turn down, fold*. See also **rabbit**.

receipt

In English, **receipt** refers to the action of *receiving something*, Swedish **mottagande**, or *a printed or written statement* that you have received something or that something has been paid for, Swedish **kvitto**. In business language, **receipts** are the money received by a business during a certain period, Swedish **intäkter, kassa**. The word comes from Latin RECEPTUM, *thing received*, from RECIPERE, *to receive*. Of the same origin, **recept** in English means *an idea or image formed in the mind by repeated exposure to a particular stimulus*.

The Swedish word **recept** has two meanings: *recipe* and *a doctor's prescription*. It has the same Latin origin as **receipt**.

In the 14th century, both **receipt** and **recipe** referred to medicine. There is not much difference between preparing medicine and preparing food—in both cases it is a matter of preparing ingredients—so, in the 18th century, **recipe** began to be used also in the kitchen.

reclaim

Reclaim means *to regain, recover,* or *recycle,* in Swedish **återvinna**. The word comes from Old French RÉCLAMER, *to call back,* from Latin RECLAMARE, *to shout back, cry out against.*

Reklam in Swedish is *advertising* or *publicity*. It has the same Latin origin as the English word—and don't you sometimes feel as if advertising is shouting at you?

reclamation

This English word is a noun that is related to **reclaim** and means *claiming something back,* such as land formerly under water, or *obtaining useful materials from waste products,* Swedish **återvinning**. The original Latin word RECLAMATIO meant *a shout of disapproval,* from the verb RECLAMARE, *to cry out against.*

In Swedish, with the same origin, **reklamation** means *complaint*. If you have bought something that does not work, you can **reklamera** or put in a **reklamation**, even if you don't necessarily have to shout disapprovingly.

rector

In the Church of England, a **rector** is *a priest in charge of a parish,* Swedish **kyrkoherde**, in the Roman Catholic Church *a priest in charge of a church or a religious institution*. A **rector** is also *the head of certain universities, colleges,* *and schools*. In Scotland, a **rector** is an *elected representative of the students on a university's governing body*.

Rektor in Swedish refers to *a headmaster or headmistress* at a school. A **rektor** of a university in Sweden is the equivalent of *a vice-chancellor* in the UK or *a president* or *chancellor* in the USA.

Rector and **rektor** come from Latin RECTOR, *ruler*, from the verb REGERE, *to rule*.

red

This English word for the *colour* of blood or strawberries, from Latin RUBER, *red*, is **röd** in Swedish.

The Swedish word **rädd** is pronounced like **red**. It means *afraid, scared* and comes from Old Swedish RÆDDER, *frightened*.

red day

In English **a red day** is *a day when you have bad luck or experience something disagreeable*, Swedish **otursdag** or **Tycho Brahe-dag**. Tycho Brahe was a Danish astronomer, astrologer, and alchemist in the second half of the 16th century. He had an observatory on the now Swedish island of Ven. He developed astronomical instruments and determined the fixed positions of almost 800 stars. Brahe was appointed astronomer and astrologer of the court of emperor Rudolf II in Prague, now in the Czech Republic, where he developed a centre of astronomical studies together with his assistant Johannes Kepler. According to history, Brahe was also commissioned by the emperor to establish which days of the year could be considered **red days**. On such days it was bad luck to move house, change jobs, or get married. Tycho Brahe died in Prague in 1601.

In old folklore, going back to ancient civilizations, certain days in the year were considered to be especially unlucky. *Bondepraktikan*, the old *Farmer's Almanac* in Sweden, listed 33 such days in the year.

In the United States, the **National Wear Red Day**® brings attention to heart disease as a leading cause of death for Americans. The United Kingdom also has a **Wear Red Day**, an annual event launched by the Children's Heart Surgery Fund. Another **Wear Red Day** in the UK tackles racism in society. The main idea, taken from football, is to show racism the red card.

Red day alludes to the colour of blood and is a euphemism for a *day when a woman is menstruating*.

In Swedish, **röd dag** refers to *a Sunday* or *a national or public holiday*. Such days are marked red in calendars. In the United Kingdom, public holidays are also called **bank holidays**.

regime

From Latin REGIMEN, *rule*, via French RÉGIME, the word refers to *a government*, particularly an authoritarian one, Swedish **regim**, or *a system of doing things*, often a coordinated programme for the promotion of health, also called a **regimen**, Swedish **levnadsregler**.

In Swedish, **regim** refers to *government* or *leadership*, and **regimen** is the definite form of the word, *the government*.

rentable

Rentable means that something, e.g., an office space, is *suitable or available for renting*, Swedish **uthyrningsbar**. The word is formed from RENT and ABLE. **Rent** is from Vulgar Latin RENDERE, a combination of REDDERE, *to give back*, and PRENDERE, *to take*.

Räntabel in Swedish means *profitable*. It comes from French RENTABLE.

reparation

Reparation comes from the Latin word REPARARE, meaning *to make ready again, put back in order*. In English, **reparation** means *compensation, indemnity*, which is **ersättning, skadestånd** in Swedish.

The Swedish noun **reparation** has retained the Latin sense of *repairing, mending*.

repetition

Repetition means *the act of doing or saying again*, which was also the sense of the original Latin REPETITIONEM.

In Swedish, **repetition** also means *rehearsal*. **Generalrepetition** corresponds to the English **dress rehearsal**.

representation

This English word means *portrayal, depiction, symbol*, etc. It also refers to *speaking or acting on behalf of somebody*. Corresponding Swedish words would be **framställning** or **skildring**, and **representation**, respectively. The word comes from Latin REPRAESENTARE, *to make present, show*.

In Swedish, **representation** is often equivalent to *entertaining* in the sense of (usually a company) having clients or business associates as guests and providing them with food, drink, and entertainment.

resign

When you **resign**, you voluntarily *leave your job*, Swedish **avgå, säga upp sig**. The word comes from Latin RE-, *back*, and SIGNARE, *to sign, seal*. RESIGNARE consequently meant *to unseal* or *cancel*. You can also **resign** to something, accept that something unwanted cannot be avoided, Swedish **acceptera**.

In Swedish, **resignera** has the latter meaning, *to give up, to accept one's fate*.

rest

The English verb **rest** means *to stop doing something in order to relax*. The word is of Germanic origin from a root meaning *league* or *mile*, referring to a distance after which one rests. The corresponding noun **rest** refers to *a period of time when you rest* or *the state you are in when you rest*. Both the verb **rest** and the noun **rest** are **vila** in Swedish.

Another noun **rest** means *what is left, remainder, the remaining part*. The origin is Latin RESTARE, stand back.

In Swedish, **rest** refers to *what is left*. The word is also the third form, the perfect participle, of the verb **resa**, *travel*.

restroom

In US English, **restroom** is a euphemism for *toilet*. There are other words for toilet in English: *bathroom, comfort station, gents', john, ladies', lavatory, loo, powder room, privy, the smallest room, washroom*, etc. The most common Swedish word for this is **toalett**, in familiar language often abbreviated **toa**. **WC**, short for **water closet**, is also used in Swedish.

Toilet comes from French TOILETTE, small tablecloth, from TOILE, *cloth, tissue*.

Other euphemisms for going to the toilet in English are phrases such as **wash your hands** and **powder your nose**. A guest in a British home might be told **'I'll show you where you can wash your hands'** and may think that his host thinks that he is dirty. A British friend of mine told me that she had said, **'I need to powder my nose'** when visiting a family in Sweden, and her hostess had taken a close look at her and then said, **'No, you don't. It's perfectly fine.'**

Other phrases about going to the toilet are **'I've got to see a man about a horse'**, **'I've got to see a man about a dog'**, or **'I've got to see a man about the plumbing'**. The first two refer to betting on a horse race or a dog race.

If you have guests from Sweden, they might ask you if they may **borrow your toilet**. You needn't worry—they just want to use it, but they do not know that the correct English expression is **May I use your bathroom?**

A colloquial Swedish word for toilet is **mugg**, *mug*. **Gå på muggen** means *go to the loo*. **Dass** is an old Swedish word for *toilet*, usually an outdoor one. It comes from German DAS HAUS, *the house*.

Bajamaja is Swedish for *portaloo, portable toilet*, often used at outdoor festivals, campsites, and construction sites.

Rest in **restroom** means *relaxation, repose, sleep,* Swedish **vila**. The word originally meant just that, a *room set aside for rest and quiet*, but in the 1930s it became a euphemism for **toilet**. Consequently, the word is easily misinterpreted by Swedes, who are guided by the word **rest** in **restroom**. An American was picking up his Swedish friend at an airport, and when they got into the car, the American said, **'Perhaps you need to go to the restroom?'**, and without hesitating, the Swede answered, **'No, I can do that in the car.'**

See also **Loo**.

reverse

In English, the verb **reverse** means *to move backwards*, Swedish **backa**, or *to change something into the opposite of what it originally was*, Swedish **ändra**. **Reverse** can also be used as a noun, an adjective, or an adverb, all referring to the notion of *backwards* or *opposite*. The word comes from Latin RE-, *back*, and VERTERE, *to turn* (see also **backside**).

The Swedish noun **revers** refers to *a promissory note*, i.e., a signed document with a promise to pay a certain sum of money to a certain person at a certain date. The word comes from Middle Latin REVERSUM, *returned*.

road

As everybody knows, a **road** is *a long piece of hard ground* for people to drive on to move from one place to another. The Swedish word is **väg** (related to English **way**). **Road** comes from Old English RÁD, *to ride*.

The Swedish word **road** (with a different pronunciation) is the past participle of **roa**, *to amuse, entertain*. **Roa** is related to **ro**, *rest, peace*, which comes from Germanic ROWO.

rock

The English word **rock** has several meanings. It refers to *the solid mineral material* that is a part of the surface of the Earth or a large mass of this protruding above the surface of the Earth. It can also mean *a large piece of rock* that has become detached from a mountain. This **rock** comes from medieval Latin ROCCA. Corresponding Swedish words are **klippa** and **berg**.

A diamond is sometimes called a **rock**. A **rock** is also a kind of cylindrical hard *confectionery*.

Rock is *a music genre*, originally called **rock-and-roll**. Related to jazz music, **rock** originated in America.

Gibraltar is informally known as **the Rock**. Situated at the inlet of the Mediterranean Sea, the 450 m high limestone rock is a famous landmark.

As a verb, **rock** means *to move gently from side to side*. It can also refer to a stronger action, such as when an earthquake rocks a city.

When something is very good or works very well, you can say that **it rocks**.

In Swedish, in addition to referring to music, **rock**, from Old High German ROC, means *overcoat*. **Städrock** is *overall* in UK English and *duster* in American English.

S

sambo

This North American English word is an old taboo word for *a black person* or *mulatto*. The word comes from a Spanish term for a person of African or Native American ancestry.

Sambo in Swedish refers to a common-law husband or wife, *a cohab* or *cohabitee*, from SAMMAN, *together*, and BO, *to live*.

scam

In English, **scam** is *a fraud, a dishonest scheme*. The verb means *to swindle*. Its origin is unknown. The Swedish noun is **bluff, svindleri, lurendrejeri**, and the verb is **lura, svindla**.

Skam in Swedish means *shame* or *disgrace*. The word is possibly from Old High German SCAMA, *cover, wrap*.

scat

Scat is *a way of singing* in jazz with the voice imitating the sound of a musical instrument. The American trumpet player Louis Armstrong (1901–1971) was a master of scat singing.

Scat is also *an interjection*, meaning *Go away!*, possibly from SCATTER.

Skatt in Swedish has different meanings: *tax, treasure,* or *darling*. The word is related to Old High German SCAZ and Old English SCEATT, *coin, money*.

schema

From Greek SKHEMA, *form, figure,* this word is used in English as a term in philosophy and logic, *an outline or model of a theory*.

Schema in Swedish, of the same Greek origin, usually means *timetable, schedule*, but it can also refer to *a circuit diagram*.

scum

Scum is *a film or layer of dirt or froth* on a liquid, Swedish **hinna** or **skum**. The verb **scum** means *to remove scum*, Swedish **skumma**. The noun is also a derogatory word for *a worthless or contemptible person*, Swedish **avskum**. **Scum** probably comes from Proto-Germanic *SKUMAZ, *froth, foam,* and *dark*, from a Proto-Indo-European *(S)KEWH-, *to cover, conceal*.

With the same origin, the Swedish noun **skum** means *foam* or *spray*. Unlike English **scum**, this noun does not necessarily imply something dirty.

The Swedish adjective **skum**, probably of the Proto-Indo-European root mentioned above, means *darkish, obscure,* and (about people and activities) *shady, suspicious*.

Secretary of State

In the UK, a **Secretary of State** is *the head of a major department*, Swedish **departementschef, minister, statsråd**; in the USA, the **Secretary of State** is *the foreign minister*, Swedish **utrikesminister**.

Statssekreterare in Swedish corresponds to a British *Under-secretary of State*.

self-conscious

English **conscious** and its Swedish translation **medveten** both mean *aware of or having knowledge about something*. In late 16th century English, **conscious** meant *being aware of wrongdoing*. CONSCIUS in Latin meant *knowing with others or in oneself*. **Self-conscious** refers to *an awareness about oneself*, especially in connection with how others might perceive one's appearance or actions. This may lead to low self-esteem, shyness, or even paranoia. **Self-conscious** in Swedish is **förlägen, osäker**.

The Swedish word **självmedveten** has the opposite meaning of *self-confident* or *self-assured*.

semester

Latin SEMESTRIS referred to *six months*. Holders of public offices in ancient Rome had a tenure of six months. The word SEMESTRE was used in France in the 18th century to denote the holiday period granted to military officers. In English it refers to *a study period* at schools and universities. In the USA there are two **semesters** (spring and fall); in the UK they are called **terms** and there are three (autumn, spring, and summer). This meaning of *study period* comes from German **SEMESTER**. English **semester** is **termin** in Swedish.

In Sweden, **semester** means *holiday* or *vacation*. However, a Swedish vacation is not six months long, but at least five weeks (with pay).

sensible

If you are **sensible** in English, you are *reasonable, judicious,* or *wise*. The word can also mean *practical* or *noticeable*. Coming from Latin **SENTIRE**, *to feel*, in the late 14th century the word meant *capable of sensation or feeling*. **Sensible** is **förnuftig, klok** in Swedish.

The Swedish word **sensibel** corresponds to *sensitive* in English.

set

Set in English has several meanings. As a verb, it means *to put something in a certain place* or position, Swedish **sätta, ställa, lägga**, *to establish something*, or *to fix*, for example, a date, Swedish **bestämma**. This **set** is of Germanic origin, related to German **SETZEN** and Dutch **SETTEN**.

The adjective **set** means *arranged in advance, ready*, Swedish **klar, färdig**, and the noun **set** means *a group of similar things or people*, Swedish **uppsättning**, *a part of a game of tennis* and other games, Swedish **set**, and *a collection of stage furniture* and other things used for a scene in a film or play, Swedish **dekor**. The noun **set** comes from Latin SECTA, *sect*, via Old French SETTE.

Set is used in Swedish to denote *a part of a game of tennis* and other games and *a collection of things*. The Swedish word **sätt** means *method, way*, or *behaviour, manner*. **Sätt!** is the imperative of **sätta**, *to put*.

sex

The English noun **sex** refers to either of the two categories of most living beings, *male or female*. The word also means *sexual activity*, particularly sexual intercourse. The origin is Old French SEXE or Latin SEXUS, *sex, gender*.

The Swedish word **sex** also refers to *sexual activity*, but the word is also a numeral, *the number six*, from Proto-Indo-European *SWÉKS and Proto-Germanic *SWEHS.

silicon

Silicon is *a non-metal* with semiconducting properties, atomic number 14, symbol Si, Swedish **kisel**. From Latin SILEX, *flint*, the word became SILICIUM in English and was later changed on the pattern of **carbon** to **silicon**.

Silikon, of the same origin, is the Swedish word for *silicone*, a man-made polymer used in sealants, adhesives, lubricants, etc.

simple

The adjective **simple** in English means *uncomplicated* or *easily understood*, Swedish **enkel, lätt**. Referring to a person, it can mean *humble, unpretentious*, Swedish **enkel, anspråkslös**. The word comes from Latin SIMPLUS, *single*, or SIMPLEX, *onefold, unmixed*.

In Swedish, **simpel** usually means *base, common, low*. It can also mean *vulgar*.

sin

A **sin** is *an act of evil, a transgression against divine law*, or *a serious offence*, Swedish **synd**. The verb **sin**, Swedish **synda**, means *to commit a sin*. The word is probably related to Latin SONS, *guilty*. In Old English, the noun was SYNN and the verb SYNGIAN.

Sin in Swedish, roughly pronounced as English **seen**, is a reflexive possessive pronoun, corresponding to English *his, her, its, their*, and *one's*.

single

In English, **single** can be a noun, a verb, and an adjective. The noun means *an individual thing or person*, such as an unmarried person or a single ticket, valid only for an outward journey. A **single** is also *a CD with a small amount of music* or *a tennis match* with one player on each side. The verb means *to choose something or someone* for a special purpose. The adjective means *consisting of one part* or *unmarried*. **Single** comes from Latin SINGULUS, related to SIMPLUS, *single*.

Singel in Swedish shares the English meanings related to an unmarried person, a CD record, and a tennis match. In addition, it means *shingle* or *coarse gravel* as well as a *vest* or *undershirt*.

slag

Slag, Swedish **slagg,** is *waste material separated from metals when ore is being refined*. The word probably comes from Middle Low German SLAGEN, *to strike*.

The German origin is reflected in the Swedish noun **slag,** which means a *blow, hit,* or *strike*. **Slag** in Swedish also means *kind* or *type, battle,* and *moment*. **Vänta ett slag!** is **Wait a moment!** or **Hang on!** in English.

slam

The English verb **slam** means *to shut* a door, window, etc., *loudly and forcefully,* Swedish **slå igen, smälla igen**. In informal language, **slam** means *to criticize strongly,* Swedish **göra ner, skälla ut**. The word is probably of Scandinavian origin.

Slam in Swedish means *sludge, mud,* from German SCHLAMM.

In both English and Swedish, **slam** is a term from bridge; **grand slam** is *all thirteen tricks* and **small slam** *twelve tricks*. In sport, **grand slam** refers to a *set of championships or matches in the same year,* especially in tennis.

slant

Slant in English is *a sloping position, a diversion* from a vertical or horizontal axis, Swedish **lutning**, or the corresponding verb, Swedish **luta**. It can also refer to *a biased presentation* of information, Swedish **vinkling**. The word is related to Old Norse SLENT and Swedish SLINTA, *to slip*.

In Swedish, **slant** is *a coin* or *a small amount of money*, and **slänt** is *a slope* or *hillside*. Swedish **slant** was probably a dialectal word meaning *rag*, from the verb SLANTA, *to dangle, swing*, related to SLINTA (see above).

sleep

Sleep is, of course, what we usually do during the night, *the opposite of being awake*. **Sleep** is both a verb, Swedish **sova**, and a noun, Swedish **sömn**. It comes from the German verb SCHLAFEN.

The Swedish noun **slip** is pronounced like **sleep**, but it means *slipway*, used for launching and landing boats. Another **slip** in Swedish is *a grinder*.

slip

The verb **slip** means *to slide*, Swedish **glida, halka**, *to move quickly*, Swedish **slinka iväg, kila iväg**, *to lose your hold*, Swedish **tappa greppet**, or *to get worse*, Swedish **bli sämre**. You can **slip into**, i.e., *put on*, clothes or **slip** them **off**, Swedish **dra på sig** and **dra av sig**. In Middle English SLIP meant *to move quickly and softly*.

As a noun, **slip** can refer to *a small piece of paper*. Swedish **remsa**, a *small mistake*, Swedish **lapsus, misstag**, a *fall to a lower standard*, Swedish **fall, nedgång**, or *a short petticoat*, Swedish **underkjol**.

Slip in Swedish means *slipway* as well as *grinder* (see **sleep** above). **Slips** is a *tie* or *necktie*. This word comes from German **SCHLIPS**, *coat-tail*, which is also the origin of English **slip** in the sense of *paper slip*. The Swedish verb **slippa** from Old Norse SLEPPA means *to escape, avoid, not have to do*.

slot

A **slot** is *a narrow opening or slit* in a machine, into which you can insert, for example, a coin or a credit card, Swedish **springa, öppning**. In late Middle English the word meant *a slight depression running down the middle of the chest*.

A Swedish **slott** is *a palace, castle*, or *chateau*. The word comes from Middle Low German **SLOT**, *door lock, fortified place*.

slug

A **slug** is *a small, slow-moving animal* like a snail but without a shell, Swedish **snigel**, Latin *Cochlea*. The word can also refer to *a slow person*. It is probably of Scandinavian origin. **Slug** is also an amount of drink, a *swig*, Swedish **klunk**.

In US English, a **slug** is *a bullet*, especially for an airgun, Swedish **kula**. As a verb, it means *to hit (somebody) hard*, Swedish **puckla på**.

In computing, a **slug** is a *short text*, a part of a URL (Uniform Resource Locator) that identifies a page on a website

The Swedish word **slug** is an adjective meaning *shrewd, astute,* and *sly, cunning*, of Low German origin.

slump

To **slump** is *to sit down or fall heavily* on a chair, sofa, etc., Swedish **sjunka ner**. In economics, **slump** refers to *a sudden fall in price or value*, Swedish **fall, nedgång**. The word is used both as a verb and as a noun. In the late 17th century, it meant *to fall into a bog*. The word comes from Norwegian SLUMPE, *to fall*.

A **slump** in Swedish means *coincidence, hazard, luck*. It is from Middle Low German SLUMP of the same meaning.

slut

In English this is a derogatory, disrespectful word used to say that a woman is a *prostitute* or *whore*. Other synonyms are *bitch, tramp,* or *hooker*. In Middle English SLUTTE meant *untidy woman*. The sexual connotation did not appear until the 1960s. **Slut** in English is **fnask** or **slampa** in Swedish.

The Swedish word **slut** has a completely different meaning, *end* or *ending*. On a railway line there is a **slutstation**. In the days leading up to a new year, people in Sweden wish each other **ett gott slut**, *a good ending*.

A Swedish researcher allegedly sent an academic paper labelled **slutversion**, Swedish for *final version*, to a scientific journal.

sly

If you are **sly**, you are *cunning and deceitful*, in Swedish **listig, slug**. Sly comes from Old Norse SLŒGR, *cunning*, originally *able to strike*, from SLÁ, *to strike*, from Proto-Indo-European *SLAK-, *to hit, throw*.

Sly in Swedish is a botanical word meaning *brushwood*. It is probably of Danish or Norwegian origin.

smart

This English word has several meanings. The original sense (related to German **schmerzen**) was *causing sharp pain*, Swedish **skarp, svidande**. This led to *keen, brisk*, Swedish **livlig**, and later to *mentally sharp, bright, brainy, crafty,* and *shrewd*, Swedish **begåvad, klipsk**. Another sense is *stylish, fashionable,* or *elegant*, Swedish **stilig, elegant**. **Smart** can also mean *active, lively, quick,* or *energetic*, Swedish **kvick, snabb**. As a verb, it means *to ache, hurt,* or *be painful*, Swedish **göra ont, svida**.

The Swedish word **smart** is an English loanword and only refers to *being intelligent*. The original sense of pain mentioned above is reflected in Swedish **smärta**, *pain*.

smell

Smell is a noun meaning *scent, fragrance,* or *odour,* Swedish **doft, lukt**. As a verb it means *to perceive an odour or scent* with your nose, Swedish **lukta**. Something (such as a flower) can also **smell**, that is, *emit an odour or scent,* Swedish **dofta** or **lukta**. The verb **smell** comes from Proto-Indo-European *SMEL-, *to burn, smoke, smoulder*. The noun is from Middle English SMEL.

In Swedish, the word **smäll**, pronounced just like the English word, means *bang, crash, slap,* or *impact.* **Smäll** is related to an Old English verb SMIELLAN, *to cause a bang.*

smoking

Smoking is, of course, the habit of *inhaling fumes from cigars, cigarettes, pipes, etc.* This is called **rökning** in Swedish. **Smoke** comes from a Germanic base SMEOCAN, *to emit smoke.*

In Swedish, a **smoking** is *a tuxedo* or *dinner jacket.* The word comes from English **smoking jacket**.

solution

Solution is *a way of solving a problem* or *the correct answer* to a problem, for example, in an exam. A **solution** is also *a mixture of liquids.* The origin is Latin SOLVERE, *to loosen.* In both cases, the corresponding Swedish word is **lösning**.

Swedish speakers often talk or write in English about **solution** without mentioning what the problem is. They could instead use **alternative, option, concept,** or **design** (**'We've come up with a new design'**). Swedish **lösning** can also be *an answer to a problem* in English.

spark

In English, a **spark** is *a glowing particle* emerging from a fire or from striking together two hard objects such as metal or stone, Swedish **gnista**. In a car, a **spark** ignites the mixture of fuel and air in the engine. The word is also used figuratively as in **a spark of hope** or **a spark of joy**. The word is also used as a verb. In Old English it was SPÆRKA.

A Swedish **spark** is *a kick*. Especially in northern Sweden, people use a **spark**, *a kick-sled*, in winter. The word is from Old Norse **SPARKA**, *to kick*.

speaker

A **speaker** is, of course, *someone who speaks or gives a speech*, Swedish **talare**. **Speaker** is also the title of *the presiding officer in a legislative assembly* such as the House of Commons in the UK and the House of Representatives in the USA. This corresponds to **talman** in the Swedish Parliament.

Speaker is also the abbreviation of **loudspeaker**, Swedish **högtalare**.

In Swedish, **speaker** is a loanword from English. It mainly refers to *a compère* or *an announcer* at a sports event.

speck

A **speck** is *a very small spot*, Swedish **fläck**. The word comes from Old English SPECCA. It can also be used as a verb, *to mark with small spots*.

Späck in Swedish means *animal fat* or *bacon fat*, from Middle Low German SPEK.

spectacle

Spectacle comes from Latin SPECTACULUM, *public show*. The current meaning of the English word is *a performance or display with a strong visual impact*, Swedish **skådespel, föreställning**. The adjective **spectacular** means *striking, breathtaking, amazing*, Swedish **imponerande, spektakulär**. The visual connection is also apparent in **a pair of spectacles**, which is a synonym of *eyeglasses*.

In Swedish, **spektakel** has the same Latin origin. The word refers to an action that causes attention and means *row, nuisance, scandal*, or *hullabaloo*. It can also mean *ridicule* or *laughing stock*.

spiritual

Spiritual means *connected with your spirit or with religion*. The base of this word is Latin SPIRITUS, *breath* or *spirit*, from an Indo-European verb meaning *to blow* or *breathe*. The Swedish word for **spiritual** is **andlig**.

It is interesting to note that the Swedish word for **spirit** is *ande*, and the word for **breathe** is *andas*. However, the Swedish word **spirituell** means *witty* or *brilliant*. From SPIRITUS, Swedish also has **sprit**, meaning *liquor*.

Originally, **spirituell** in Swedish also had the same meaning as English **spiritual**. The word came from 17th century French and had connotations of both wittiness and religion. In the 1900s, *witty* had become the dominant sense in Swedish. Nowadays, through English influence, **spirituell** is again used by some in the sense of **andlig**.

spot

The English noun **spot** can refer to *a dot* or *mark*, Sw. **fläck**, or *a place*, Swedish **plats**. The verb means *to notice, observe, recognize*, Swedish **upptäcka**, or *to stain*, Swedish **fläcka ner**. It is of Germanic origin, possibly related to Old Norse SPOTTI, *small piece*, or Norwegian SPOT, *small piece of land*.

In Swedish, **spott** is *saliva or spittle*. The expression **spott och spe** means *scorn and derision*. The word is of Germanic origin.

spring

As a noun, **spring** has several meanings. It is *the season between winter and summer*, Swedish **vår**. And it is *a metal coil* that will return to its previous shape after it has been pressed down, commonly used in cars and beds, Swedish **fjäder**. A third sense of **spring** is *the place where water comes up from the ground*, Swedish **källa**.

The verb **spring** means *to jump, move suddenly upwards*, Swedish **hoppa**, or *to originate or suddenly develop* from something, Swedish **uppstå, dyka upp**.

The Old English verb SPRINGAN, of Germanic origin, meant *to rush out in a stream*.

In Swedish, **springa** is a verb meaning *to run*, and **Spring!** is the imperative of that verb, *Run!* **Springa fram** means *to spring forth*.

Swedish **springa** is also a noun meaning *slot, crack, crevice*.

spy

A **spy** is *someone who tries to find out secret information* about a government, a corporation, or other organization, Swedish **spion**. **Spy** as a verb refers to that action, Swedish **spionera**. The word comes from Old French ESPIER, *to espy, catch sight of*.

Spy in Swedish is a verb meaning *to vomit, throw up*. It is of Indo-European origin and related to Old English SPIWAN, *to spew*.

stadium

Stadium in English is *a sports arena* with an area surrounded by a grandstand for spectators. The corresponding Swedish word is **stadion**, which was the original ancient Greek word for *a fixed standard of length* of footraces and *a running track*. The word became STADIUM in Latin.

In Swedish, **stadium** means *stage, phase, period*. In the nine-year compulsory school, **lågstadium** is *the junior level*, **mellanstadium** *the intermediate level*, and **högstadium** *the senior level*.

stake

A **stake** is a strong wooden or metal *pole* driven into the ground as a support for a plant or a fence, etc., Swedish **stake, stör**. The word is of West Germanic origin. In the Middle Ages, **burning at the stake** was a common punishment for heresy and other crimes. The victim was tied to a **stake**, Swedish **påle**, and a fire was lit beneath. **To be burnt at the stake** is **brännas på bål** in Swedish.

Stake as a noun or a verb also refers to *an interest in an undertaking*, Swedish **andel**, *money gambled on the outcome of a game*, Swedish **insats**, or *prize money* in, e.g., horse racing, Swedish **prispengar**.

When something is **at stake**, it is *at risk*.

The Swedish noun **stake** is used in the same sense of *pole* as the English word. In Swedish, **stake** also means *candlestick*. It can also refer to somebody's *drive* in the sense of *energy*. In vulgar Swedish, **stake** refers to *a penis* or *an erection*.

stall

The English word **stall** has several meanings. As a verb it can mean *to delay, halt, hamper, hinder, interrupt, put off, stop, suspend*, Swedish **uppehålla, hindra**; *to break down, fail*, Swedish **tjuvstanna**; *to make excuses*,

Swedish **slingra sig**, etc. The noun can mean *box, booth, cabin, cabinet, cubicle*, Swedish **bås**, and *market stand*, Swedish **stånd**. **The stalls** are *the seats on the main level of a theatre or cinema*, Swedish **parkett** or **parkettplats**.

Stall in Swedish has only one meaning, *stable*, the building where you keep horses or other livestock. The Germanic origin of **stall** is the same in English and Swedish. In Old English, STEALL meant *stable* or *cattle shed*.

stare

To **stare** means *to look fixedly* at someone or something, Swedish **stirra**, and the noun **stare** is *a long, fixed look*, Swedish **blick**. The word has a Germanic origin from a base meaning *to be fixed or rigid*.

Stare in Swedish is a bird, *starling, Sturnus vulgaris*.

stark

Stark in English means *sharply delineated, severe, straightforward*, Swedish **avskalad, ren**, or *complete, utter*, Swedish **fullständig**. It is used in phrases such as **stark raving mad**. STEARC in Old English meant *stiff, rigid, unyielding, severe*.

Stark naked comes from Middle English STERT NAKED, from STERT, *tail* (similar to the modern **butt naked**).

Swedish **stark** means *strong*. The word is from Proto-Germanic *STARKUZ and is related to Old English STEARC and Old Norse STERKR.

steak

Steak is *high-quality meat* from cattle or fish, cut into thick slices to be grilled or fried, Swedish **biff**. The word comes from Old Norse STEIK, related to STEIKJA, *to roast on a spit*.

The Swedish word **stek** (also of Norse origin) means *roast* or *joint of roast meat*. Another **stek** (from Dutch STEEK, related to Middle Low German STEKE) means *hitch* or *knot*. **Pålstek** is *a bowline [knot]*.

steal

To **steal** something is *to take it without permission*, intending to keep it. You can also **steal** another person's ideas. In sports, **steal** means *to gain an advantage*. The corresponding Swedish word is **stjäla**. A **steal** is an informal word for a *bargain*, Swedish **fynd**. In American English, a **steal** is *the act of stealing*. The verb **steal** is of Germanic origin and was STELAN in Old English.

With roughly the same pronunciation, Swedish **stil** means *style*. **Stil** comes from Latin STILUS, *rod, stick, style of writing*, from an Indo-European root.

Swedish **stel**, from Old West Norse STIRÐR, means *stiff, rigid, strict*.

steel

Steel is *a strong metal*, an alloy of iron with carbon and other elements, Swedish **stål**. The word is of Germanic origin, in Old English STYLE or STELI.

For the Swedish words **stel** and **stil**, see **steal**.

stick

The English noun **stick** means *a long, thin piece of wood* that has fallen from a tree, Swedish **pinne**, is used to help you walk, Swedish **käpp**, is used for hitting someone or something, such as the ball or puck in sports, Swedish **klubba**, or is used for playing the drums, Swedish **trumstock**. In a car, **the stick** is *the gearshift lever*, Swedish **växelspak**. The noun **stick** is of West Germanic origin and was STICCA in Old English.

As with many English words, **stick** has a number of other definitions. In addition to those mentioned above, the word can be used to denote *the clarinet* in a jazz band, *a flat-chested woman* or, but this is archaic and rare, *a quantity of eels*, usually 25.

The verb **stick** can mean *to push something into something else*, Swedish **sticka in**, or *to become fixed* in one position, Swedish **fastna**. The verb **stick** comes from an Indo-European root, in Latin INSTIGARE, *to spur on*, and in Old English STICIAN.

In Swedish, **stick** means *prick, sting, stab*. The noun **sticka** is *a splinter, sliver, matchstick*, or *a knitting-needle*. It has the same origin as English **stick**. The verb **sticka** is *to prick or sting*. It also means *to knit*. In colloquial language, **sticka** means *to go off, run off,* and the imperative **Stick!** means *Scram!* In jazz music, Swedish **stick** is *bridge* in English, usually eight bars with a significantly different melody from the rest of the song.

stock

Stock can refer to *the goods kept in a shop* for sale, Swedish **lager**, or to *a share in a company,* Swedish **aktie**. **Stock** are farm animals, especially *cattle, livestock,* Swedish **boskap**. **Stock** is also used in cooking; it is *a liquid made by cooking bones, meat, etc.,* used to make soup or gravy, Swedish **buljong**. A person's *ancestry* is also called **stock**, Swedish **härkomst**. **Stock** is also *the trunk of a tree,* Swedish **stam**. The verb **stock** means *to keep a supply of a product,* Swedish **lagra**.

As an adjective, **stock** means *usual* or *typical,* used or done so many times that it is *no longer original,* Swedish **utnött, klichéartad**. You can talk about **a stock phrase** or **stock jokes**.

Old English STOCC, of Germanic origin, meant *trunk, block of wood.*

Stock in Swedish means *log,* from Old Swedish STOKKER. **Vinstock** is *a vine.*

stool

A **stool** is *a seat* without a back or arms, Swedish **pall**. **Stool** is also *a piece of faeces,* solid waste from the anus, Swedish **avföring**. The word is of Germanic origin.

A **stool pigeon** is *a police informant*, Swedish **tjallare**, or a person acting as *a decoy*, Swedish **lockfågel**.

Stol in Swedish, of Proto-Indo-European origin, is *a chair*.

strand

Strand comes from a Proto-Indo-European word meaning *to broaden, spread out*. It got its meaning of *shore*, Swedish **strand**, from Old English.

The Strand is a street in London. Before the construction of the Victoria Embankment, it used to be close to the river Thames. A small street off the Strand to access the Savoy Hotel is the only street in the UK where you drive on the right.

The Grand Strand is the nickname of a 97 kilometres (60 miles) long beach in South Carolina, USA. Its real name Myrtle Beach is also the name of a city in the area.

The verb **strand** means *to drive aground on a shore*, Swedish **stranda**. A boat can be **stranded**, *left aground on a shore*, and a person can be **stranded**, *left without being able to move from somewhere*.

Strand has also another meaning in English. It refers to *fibres* or *filaments that are twisted together to form a thread, rope, or wire*, Swedish **tråd, rep, tåg**. You can also talk about **a strand of hair**, Swedish **hårslinga**. The word can also mean *a molecular chain* such as **a strand of DNA**, Swedish **DNA-sträng**.

Strand in Swedish only means *beach* or *shore*.

straw

The English noun **straw**, Swedish **halm**, refers to *dried stalks of grain*, especially when used as fodder for cattle or for weaving, for example, straw hats. **Straw** is also used for *thatching*, covering a roof.

Halm or **haulm** is also an English word for *straw*. **Halm** in German means *straw*.

A **straw** made of paper or plastic (or, nowadays, also pasta) is *used to suck liquid* such as a drink from a glass or bottle. The Swedish word for this is **sugrör**.

Of Germanic origin, **straw** was STREAW in Old English. It is related to the verb **strew**.

With the same pronunciation, **strå** in Swedish refers to *a single stalk of grass or grain* or a *single hair*.

strop

A **strop** is a narrow *strip of leather* used to sharpen a razor, Swedish **strigel**. The word is also a verb, Swedish **strigla**. **Strop** probably comes from Latin STROPPUS, *thong*.

In informal English, **strop** means *a bad mood, a temper*, probably a back-formation from **stroppy**, Swedish **ilsken**, which may be an abbreviation of **obstreperous**, *noisy and difficult to control*.

In Swedish, **stropp** is *a strong rubber band* used to fasten a tarpaulin, etc. It may have the same Latin origin as English **strop**.

In colloquial Swedish, a **stropp** is *a smart-ass, a haughty, condescending person*.

suck

The English verb **suck** means *to draw something in* (for example, into the mouth) by creating a vacuum. In informal language it means *to be very bad or unpleasant*. The Swedish word is **suga**. The origin is an Indo-European root.

The Swedish noun **suck** means *a sigh*. The corresponding verb is **sucka**. It may be related to **suga**.

swank

To **swank** in English is *to behave in a way that shows that you think that you are important*, in order to attract people's admiration, Swedish **snobba, göra sig viktig**. The noun **swank** refers to such behaviour, Swedish **snobbighet, snobbism**. The word emerged in the early 19th century; its origin is unknown.

Svank in Swedish refers to *a curve of the lower part of the back, a lumbar curve, a sway-back*, or in medical language, *lordosis*. The corresponding verb is **svanka**, *to be sway-backed*. The word was *SWINCAN, *to swing*, in Old High German.

sympathetic

From Greek SYM-, *with*, and PÁTHOS, *suffering*, **sympathetic** describes *someone who shares feelings of sadness* with somebody else, synonymous with *compassionate*, Swedish **förstående, medkännande**.

In Swedish, **sympatisk** means *nice, likeable, congenial, endearing, loveable*.

T

tablet

Tablet means *a flat slab of stone or wood*, especially one used for inscription, **a memorial tablet,** Swedish **minnestavla**.

In modern English, **tablet** refers to *a small portable computer* without a separate keyboard, Swedish **läsplatta** or **skrivplatta**. In North American English, **tablet** is also *a writing pad*, Swedish **skrivblock**.

Tablet is also *a pill* or *lozenge*, such as **a headache tablet**.

Tablet comes from a diminutive of Latin TABULA, *table*, via Old French TABLETE.

In Swedish, **tablett** only refers to *a pill* or *lozenge*.

tack

In English, a **tack** is *a small, broad-headed nail*, Swedish **nubb, stift.** The word also refers to *a way of stitching* when you fasten fabrics together temporarily before you sew them permanently, Swedish **tråckling**. When you *add something* to something already existing, you **tack it on**, Swedish **fästa**. **Tack** is also *a method* or *tactic*, how you deal with a problem, Swedish **metod**. The verb **tack** also means *to change the course of a boat*, Swedish **gå över stag, kryssa**. **Tack** probably comes from Old French TACHE, *clasp, large nail*.

The Swedish word **tack** means **thank you**. The word comes from Runic Swedish (Old East Norse) **þakk**, *pleasure, delight,* and is related to English **think**.

tag

A **tag** is *a label* that is attached to someone or something, Swedish **etikett, märke**, nowadays also **tagg**. The corresponding verb **tag**, *to attach or add something*, is now also a Swedish verb, **tagga**. If you are **taggad** in Swedish, you are *excited or psyched* about something that is going to happen.

Tag is from Late Middle English; it referred to *a narrow part* of a slashed garment.

Tag is also *a children's game*, in which one child chases the others and the one that is caught will be the next chaser. In Swedish this game is called **ta fatt, kull,** or **sistan**. The English word came into use in the middle of the 18th century.

In old-fashioned Swedish, **tag** is the imperative of **taga**, *to take*, from Runic Swedish TAKA. The modern form is **ta**. **Tag** can also mean *a grip* or *hold*. Another sense is *a moment* or *a while* as in **vänta ett tag**, *wait a moment*, or **lite i taget**, *a little at a time*. The word is, of course, related to English **take**.

Swedish **tagg** is *a spike* or *thorn*, from Old Swedish TAGGER, TAGGA, of uncertain origin.

take place

When something **takes place**, it *happens, occurs*. In Swedish this is **äga rum, hända**.

The Swedish expression **ta plats** has different meanings, *to sit down, take a seat; take up space, fill up; sit on [a committee], go into [management], take a seat [in parliament]*.

tall

Tall in English means *of more than average height*. The word is also used with measurements, **He was just a little over five feet tall**. Swedes may mistakenly use the word **long** instead, since Swedish **lång** means both *tall* and *long*.

Tall probably comes from Old English GETÆL, *prompt, swift*. The word also meant *handsome* and *bold, strong*.

Tall in Swedish is *a pine* or *fir-tree*, Latin *Pinus sylvestris*. Another Swedish word for this tree is **fur** or **fura**. In modern Swedish, **tall** is used about the tree and **fur** or **furu** about the wood or timber.

The word **tall** for the tree seems to exist in no other Germanic languages than Swedish and Norwegian.

See also **fur**.

tax

In English, **tax**, Swedish **skatt**, is *a sum of money* that people and businesses must pay to the state, based on their income or profit. A **tax** can also be added to goods or services, value-added tax or VAT, Swedish **moms**. The word also means *a strain or heavy demand* on someone, Swedish **börda, påfrestning**. The word is also used as a verb. The Latin word TAXARE meant *to censure, charge, compute*.

In Swedish, **tax** is *a dachshund,* which is a German word meaning *badger dog*. The verb **taxera** means *to rate, estimate* and particularly *assess for taxes*.

technique

Technique in English refers to *how you carry out* a particular task, an efficient way of achieving something or the skill needed to do so. To swim fast, for example, you need a good **technique**. The original Greek word TÉCHNE meant *art, skill,* from the root in Sanskrit TÁKSATI, *to build, construct*.

Swedish **teknik** has the same origin and the same meaning, but **teknik** also refers to *technology* and *engineering*.

tick

In English, this word has several meanings. **Tick** is the regular *sound of a clock* marking seconds. The word is also a verb denoting what the clock does, Swedish **ticka**.

If you say about a person, **I'd like to know what makes him tick**, it means that you want to know *what motivates him*.

Another sense of **tick** is *a mark* used to indicate that an item in a list is correct or has been selected or dealt with. As a verb, **tick** means *to mark something as correct*, etc. **This ticks all the boxes** means that *all the necessary requirements have been fulfilled*.

The Swedish verb for marking something as correct, selected, etc., corresponding to **tick** in English, is **kryssa för**, which in English means **mark with a cross**. In English you **cross out** something that is *wrong or not selected*. If you tick a box in Swedish, you mark it as wrong.

English:	Swedish:
☑ correct, selected	☑ wrong
☒ wrong	☒ correct, selected

However, the tick mark is used in Sweden to tick off items on, for example, an inventory list. Accountants tick off sums that they have checked in financial accounts.

Tick is of Germanic origin, related to Dutch TIK, TIKKEN, *pat, touch*. In Late Middle English, the noun meant *a light tap*.

Tick in English is also *a small arachnid* that sucks blood from people or animals, Swedish **fästing**; one species is called *Ixodes ricinus* in Latin. It can transmit diseases. The word is related to Dutch TEEK and German ZECKE.

As mentioned above, **ticka** in Swedish is a verb that denotes *what the clock does* when marking seconds.

The Swedish noun **ticka** is a fungus, Latin *Polyporus*, that often grows on trees.

tide

Tide in English refers to *the rising and falling of the sea* caused by the attraction of the moon and the sun, Swedish **tidvatten**. It is also used figuratively about *a strong surge* of, for example, a feeling. The word is of Germanic origin; in Old English it was TID, *time, period, era*. The reference to the sea dates from Late Middle English.

Tid in Swedish has the same meaning as the Old English word, *time, period, era*.

torn

Torn is the third form of the verb **tear** (tear – tore – torn). The verb means *to pull something apart, rip up*, Swedish **riva sönder**. **Torn**, from Old English GETOREN, is of Germanic origin.

Torn in Swedish means *tower*. It comes from Middle Low German TOREN, originally from Latin TURRIS.

trousers

Trousers are *a piece of clothing covering the lower part of the body* including the legs, Swedish **byxor**. The word comes from Irish TRIÚS and Scottish

Gaelic TRIUBHAS. In American English, **trousers** are called **pants**, which in British English are **underpants** or **underwear**.

The Swedish word **trosor** refers to women's underwear, *panties, briefs* or, colloquially, *knickers* in British English. **Trosor** probably comes from French TROUSSE, *short tight pantyhose for acrobats*, but also *case, box, kit*.

See also **pant**.

trust

A **trust** is *a strong belief*, for example, that a person is speaking the truth or is able to do something, Swedish **förtroende, tillit**. The word is also a verb, *to have confidence in*, Swedish **lita på, tro på**.

A **trust** is also an arrangement by which the owner of a property hands it over to another person or entity who must use it for the benefit of another person or other persons (beneficiaries). This is in Swedish **stiftelse**.

Trust came into Middle English from Old West Norse TRAUST, from TRAUSTR, *strong*.

The Swedish word **trast** has the same pronunciation as **trust**, but it refers to a bird, *thrush*, Latin *Turdus*.

Tröst is Swedish for *comfort, consolation, solace*, or *reassurance*. It has the same Old West Norse origin as **trust**.

U

ugly

The English word **ugly**, meaning *unattractive, disagreeable,* or *causing disquiet,* comes from Old Norse UGGLIGR, which meant *to be dreaded.* **Ugly** in Swedish is **ful, otäck**.

Uggla in Swedish means *owl,* Latin *Strix.* The word comes from a word stem that imitates the sound of the bird. Uggla as a verb is used in the phrase **sitta och uggla**, *to sit up late, doing nothing.*

under

Under in English means *below, on a lower level.* It comes from the stem of Sanskrit ADHÁH, *down, below.*

The Swedish word **under** has the same sense of *below,* but it also corresponds to English **during**.

As a noun, Swedish **under** means *wonder, marvel, miracle.* Of unknown origin, it corresponds to Old English WUNDOR.

unlucky

See **luck**

unruly

Unruly is an English adjective meaning *disorderly, uncontrollable, disobedient*, etc., Swedish **bångstyrig, oregerlig**. The word comes from Middle English UN-, *not*, and RULY, *amenable to discipline*. **Ruly** is related to **rule**.

A Swedish speaker might mistake **unruly** for **orolig**, which means *worried, concerned, restless*, etc. **O-** in Swedish corresponds to English **un-**, but the curious thing is that when you take away **o-**, you are left with the word **rolig**, which now means *funny, amusing*, and *hilarious*. Up to the end of the 1600s, ROLIG meant *calm, peaceful*—**ro** is Swedish for *peace, quiet, tranquillity*. In Danish and Norwegian, **rolig** still means *calm* and *peaceful*. The old verb **roa** originally meant *to rest, calm down*, but its modern Swedish sense is *to amuse*.

uproar

Uproar is *a tumult, loud noise or disturbance*, or *loud protest*, Swedish **kalabalik, tumult, rabalder**. The word comes from Middle Dutch OP, *up*, and ROER, *confusion*.

Uppror in Swedish (of the same origin as **uproar**) means *rebellion, insurrection, mutiny*, etc. but also, figuratively, *excitement, agitation, commotion*. It comes from Middle Low German ROR, *movement*.

V

VA

This abbreviation in English may stand for **Vice-Admiral, Vicar Apostolic, Victoria and Albert Museum** or **virtual assistant**. In the USA, **VA** stands for the state of **Virginia** or **Veterans Affairs**.

VA in Swedish is the abbreviation of **vatten och avlopp**, *drainage and water supply*.

van

A **van** is a motor vehicle used for transporting goods, Swedish **skåpbil**. It is also an abbreviation of **caravan**, a vehicle towed by a car and used for holidays, Swedish **husvagn**. Originally **caravan**, from Persian KARWAN, meant *a group of people travelling together across a desert*. In the sense of *covered horse-drawn wagon*, it is from the 19th century.

In Swedish, **van** is an adjective meaning *practiced, skilled, used to,* or *wont*. It comes from Old West Norse VANR.

VD

In English, **VD** is the abbreviation of *venereal disease*, a sexually transmitted disease (which is abbreviated STD).

VD in Swedish is short for **verkställande direktör**, *managing director*. The corresponding abbreviation in English is **CEO**, *Chief Executive Officer*.

vest

Mainly in British English, a **vest** is a man's sleeveless *undershirt*, Swedish **undertröja**. A **vest** is also a sleeveless *garment used for protection*, such as a **life vest** or **life jacket**. **Vest** comes from Latin VESTIS, *garment*, via French VESTE.

In the USA and Canada, a **vest** is what is called a **waistcoat** in British English, i.e., a sleeveless garment worn over a shirt and tie and under a jacket, typically as part of a formal three-piece suit. A Swedish **väst** corresponds to *waistcoat*. **A life jacket** is in Swedish **flytväst** or **räddningsväst**.

The verb **vest** means *to give authority* or a particular right to somebody, Swedish **överlåta**.

In Swedish, **väst** or **väster** is also one of the four principal compass directions, *west*. **Väst** and **west** come from sailors' language in Middle Low German.

See also **west**.

vicar

A **vicar** is *a member of the clergy*, an incumbent of a parish, Swedish **kyrkoherde** (literally *church shepherd*). In the Roman Catholic Church, a **vicar** is *a representative or deputy of a bishop*, Swedish **ställföreträdare**. The Pope is called **the Vicar of Christ**.

Vicar comes from Latin VICARIOUS, *substitute*, which is reflected in the Swedish word **vikarie** meaning *deputy, substitute, fill-in,* or *supply teacher*.

vice

Vice in English, from Latin VITIUM, refers to *immoral or wicked behaviour* or *criminal activities involving prostitution or drugs*, Swedish **last, synd,** and **sedlighetsbrott**, respectively.

Vice also refers to *a shortcoming, deficiency,* or *imperfection*, Swedish **svaghet, brist**.

Another **vice** in English is *a metal tool* with movable jaws used to hold an object in place while work is done on it, Swedish **skruvstäd**. This word comes from Latin VITIS, *vine*.

Vice also denotes *next in rank, deputy*, as in **vice president**, etc. The origin of this word is Latin VICE, *in place of*.

In Swedish, **vice** only means *next in rank, deputy*.

villa

A **villa** in English is *a large and luxurious country house* (esp. in continental Europe), Swedish **sommarvilla**. In the UK, it is *a large, detached house* in a residential area, especially from Victorian or Edwardian time. **Villa** can also refer to *a large country house of Roman times* with farm and residential buildings around a courtyard. The word comes from Latin VILLA, *manor, country estate*.

In Swedish, **villa** refers to *a one-family house* or *a bungalow*.

Villa or **synvilla** in Swedish means *illusion* or *delusion*. It comes from Middle Low German WILDE, *roaming*.

visa

A **visa** in English is *a permit to enter or stay in a country* for a specified period, Swedish **visum**. The word comes from Latin VISA, past participle of VIDERE, *to see*.

Visa in Swedish is a verb, *to show*, from Old English WISIAN, related to **wise**. The original sense was *to make wise, inform*. **Visa** is also the plural form of the adjective **vis**, *wise*.

Swedish **visa** is also a noun, *a song, ballad,* or *ditty*. This word is related to Old English WISE, WIS, *way, manner*, referring to the way of presenting a melody.

Swedish **vis** means both *wise* and *manner*.

visit

To **visit** is *to go and spend time with someone* or *stay temporarily as a guest or tourist*, Swedish **besöka, hälsa på**. Visit is also the corresponding noun, Swedish **besök, visit**. Latin VISITARE meant *to go and see*.

The Swedish noun **visit** has the same meaning as the English noun, but the Swedish verb **visitera** means *to frisk, search somebody down*.

vital

Vital comes from Latin VITA, *life*. This sense of the word is retained in synonyms such as *lively* and *vivacious*. The meaning *essential* emerged in the early 1600s. Some synonyms are *crucial, decisive, essential, critical*, and *necessary*. Swedish equivalents are **livsviktig, avgörande, väsentlig, kritisk, nödvändig**.

In Swedish, **vital** mainly means *energetic, active, vigorous, resilient*, or *momentous*.

W

warehouse

English synonyms for **warehouse** are *store, depository,* and *goods depot,* Swedish **lager** or **lagerlokal**. The word comes from Middle English WARES, *manufactured goods,* and HOUSE.

Varuhus in Swedish means *department store.*

way

Way in English has several meanings. It refers to *a route or direction, a distance, a method or manner, a usual behaviour, a choice from among several possibilities,* etc. **Way**, like so many English words, is of Germanic origin, related to German **Weg** and Swedish **väg**.

English **way** is more abstract than Swedish **väg**, which usually means *road*.

west

West is *the direction* in which the sun goes down or the part of a town or region that is in that direction. **The West**, Swedish **Västern** mainly refers to *North America and the European countries* that did not have communist regimes after the Second World War. **The Wild West**, Swedish **Vilda**

västern, was the part of the USA *west of the Mississippi river*. If something **goes west**, it is *damaged or lost*, Swedish **går åt helsike**.

West is a Germanic word from an Indo-European root that is found in Latin VESPER, *evening*.

Väst or **väster** in Swedish means the same as **west**, but the word **väst** is also a *waistcoat*.

See also **vest**.

will

In English **will**, from an Indo-European root, in Old English WYLLAN and German WOLLEN, is a verb that expresses the future tense, Swedish **ska, skall**, or **kommer att**. As a noun, **will** refers to *a desire* or *intention*, Swedish **vilja, avsikt**. It can also mean *a legal document* with instructions about what should be done with a person's money and property after his or her death, often referred to as the person's **last will**, Swedish **testamente**.

In Swedish, **vill** means *wish, want to*. So, if you ask a Swedish speaker, '**Will you be there?**', you may get the confusing answer, '**Yes, I will, but I can't come**'.

wink

To **wink** is *to quickly close and open one* eye as a signal of affection or greeting or to indicate that something is a joke or a secret, Swedish blinka. The word comes from Old English WINCIAN, *to close the eyes*, which is related to German **winken,** *to wave.*

This German origin lives on in Swedish, where **vinka** means *to wave, beckon.* The Swedish noun **vink** is *a hint.*

worm

In Old English, WYRM meant *worm* or *snake.* Now **worm** refers to *a small animal with a long body without arms or legs,* Swedish **mask.** The word comes from Latin VERMIS. It can also be used as a verb; you can **worm your way** by crawling and wriggling through a narrow passage, Swedish **åla sig, slingra sig.**

In modern English, **worm** can also refer to a type of self-replicating *computer virus.* It is also an acronym for a data memory device, *write-once read-many.*

Swedish **orm** means *snake.* It is related to English **worm** and has the same Latin origin. The German word for **worm, Wurm,** has given rise to Swedish **vurm,** which means *passion, craze, mania.*

wrist

The **wrist** is the joint that connects your hand with your forearm. It is probably related to the verb **writhe,** *to twist* and comes from Old German WRISTIZ. The corresponding Swedish word is **handled** (literally *hand joint*).

In Swedish, **vrist** means *instep* or *ankle*. It has the same Old German origin as the English word but relates to the foot and not to the hand.

Y

you

You is *the second-person pronoun* in English, referring to the person or persons that the speaker is addressing, Swedish **du** (singular) and **ni** (plural). **You** can also refer to any person in general, Swedish **man**. **You** comes from Old English EOW, dative and accusative of GE, later YE.

The Swedish interjection **jo**, with the same pronunciation as **you**, is used as an answer to a negative or doubting question in the sense of *oh, yes*. **Didn't you find the book? – Oh, yes, I did**, Swedish **Jo, det gjorde jag**. The word is probably related to **ja**, English **yea**, **yes**, from an Indo-European pronoun meaning *assuredly, truly*.

Conclusion

I wrote this book to help you avoid making embarrassing or even disastrous mistakes when communicating in English and Swedish, and I hope you have found it both interesting and useful. If it has made you more observant about English–Swedish false friends, it has fulfilled its aim. You might even recommend it to friends and colleagues.

If you feel like letting others know what you think about the book, you can write a review on the book's page on Amazon. Click **ratings** next to the stars and, on the next page, choose **Write a customer review**.

In your review you could consider some of the following questions:

What was the author's purpose in writing the book?
Did the author accomplish that purpose?
What makes the book special or worthwhile?
Is the book interesting? Did you find it useful?
Do you think other people would like the book?
Who would benefit from the book?

If you'd like to contact me about the book, to comment on it, to point out inadvertencies or errors, or to suggest words to be included in a future edition, send an email to medium@bahnhof.se. On my website https://copyeditor.se/books-on-the-english-language you can keep updated on coming books.

Printed in Poland
by Amazon Fulfillment
Poland Sp. z o.o., Wrocław

35724127R00133